THE BEST SCENES
FOR KIDS AGES 7–15
THE APPLAUSE ACTING SERIES

THE BEST SCENES FOR KIDS AGES 7–15
THE APPLAUSE ACTING SERIES

Edited by

Lawrence Harbison

APPLAUSE
THEATRE & CINEMA BOOKS
An Imprint of Hal Leonard Corporation

Published in 2015 by Applause Theatre & Cinema Books
An Imprint of Hal Leonard Corporation
7777 West Bluemound Road
Milwaukee, WI 53213

Trade Book Division Editorial Offices
33 Plymouth St., Montclair, NJ 07042

Printed in the United States of America

Book design by Lynn Bergesen

Library of Congress Cataloging-in-Publication Data is available upon request.

ISBN: 978-1-4950-1179-5

www.applausebooks.com

Contents

M=Male role
F=Female role

Introduction

This anthology contains fifty challenging scenes for kids. All have subject matter appropriate for production in schools, much of it "serious and challenging," which will, I believe, interest child performers without offending administrators, teachers, or parents. Some scenes are comic (laughs), some are dramatic (no laughs), and some are seriocomic (some laughs).

There are scenes here by veteran playwrights such as Don Nigro, Jenny Lyn Bader, Eric Coble, Constance Congdon, Arlene Hutton, Jack Neary, Kermit Frazier and Carlos Murillo, and by exciting up-and-comers such as Cassandra Lewis, Reina Hardy, Deanna Alisa Ableser, Martha Patterson, Mark Lambeck, and Merridith Allen. Some are from plays, but many are original pieces written for this book. The age of each character is given in each scene, but many can be done by kids not that age—so don't let the written age deter you if you like and want to use the scene.

Break a leg!

Lawrence Harbison
Brooklyn, NY

Alternative Education

Paola Soto Hornbuckle

Seriocomic

ELLIE: 13 to 15
ROBERT: 13 to 15
EVAN: 13 to 15
HANNAH: 13 to 15

Four teenagers are working on a project after school in an empty classroom. They are struggling students in Alternative Education. ELLIE is the best student and is trying to organize them. She is holding a paper.

ELLIE: All right, let's focus on our project! So . . . in Henry David Thoreau's *On Walden Pond*, we learned that Thoreau lived alone in a cottage in the woods for two whole years. Just to learn about himself. Even though he was a Harvard graduate, friends with Emerson and Hawthorne, and everyone thought he would succeed . . . he didn't. At least not at first. He quit his teaching job after two weeks and went to Walden Pond to be at one with nature. To learn about the trees, the stars . . . and how to grow beans. He really liked beans. He said, "If a man does not keep pace with his companions, perhaps it is because he hears a different drummer. Let him step to the music which he hears, however measured or far away." Mr. Von Seggern wants us each to write a paragraph about Thoreau's ideas. Any thoughts?

ROBERT: Thoreau sucks!

ELLIE: Robert, that attitude is not going to help us get an A.

ROBERT: So?

EVAN: Yeah . . . Thoreau sucks! He's boring! Do you think he ever got a girl to go out on a date with him?

ELLIE: Probably not. That's why he went to Walden Pond and hung out with the beans . . . but really? Hearing your own drummer? Being a nonconformist . . . you guys don't relate to that? I kind of see where he is going with this. It's about being true to yourself.

HANNAH: Robert made me spill my nail polish, and now my nails are ruined!

ELLIE: Hannah, Mr. Von Seggern is nice enough to let us use his room after school and if you ruin his desks we're all going to get in big trouble.

HANNAH: Like I care.

EVAN: Put it away Hannah, or Mr. Von Seggern is going to call your mother.

HANNAH: My mother is in Kansas taking care of my grandma. She just got out of rehab. I haven't seen her for a month. I'm actually staying over at Sushi's house.

ELLIE: Sushi? She hasn't been in class in weeks. I thought she ran away. What's she been up to?

HANNAH: She's kind of down. Really depressed.

ELLIE: What happened?

HANNAH: Well, her mother tried to kill her father, because she caught him cheating with another woman . . . and she shot him.

ROBERT: BANG! Yeah, she blasted his head off . . . !!

EVAN: He's missing an ear now. It's so sick! Just has a hole that oozes blood and some watery liquid.

HANNAH: Yeah, he survived, but he's like in and out of the hospital and like now her mother is in jail . . . but her brother Mike is taking care of her . . . and I'm staying with them.

ELLIE: Mike? I thought Mike was schizophrenic. He was hearing voices all semester.

ROBERT: Yeah, but they let him out of the institution for good behavior. He hasn't set a cat on fire in over a year.

EVAN: Mike's cool, man. Me and him, we're tight.

ELLIE: That's too bad. Sushi is going to fail the class. I definitely don't want to fail. I want to get an A.

HANNAH: Like she cares.

ROBERT: I'm bored! I want to leave . . . let's go to the 7-Eleven.

ELLIE: No! We need to start on our paragraphs.

[ELLIE *taps* ROBERT *on the shoulder.*]

ROBERT: You touched me! That's sexual harassment.

EVAN: Ohhhhh, she touched him . . . woowoowooo! I'm telling Mr. Von Seggern.

HANNAH: Shut up already!

ELLIE: Yes . . . good idea. Let's get to work. Let's get out a pencil and paper and talk about the assignment.

ROBERT: I don't have paper.

[ELLIE *hands him a piece of paper.*]

EVAN: I left my pencil at my dad's girlfriend's uncle's house.

[ELLIE *hands him a pencil.*]

HANNAH: I forgot my book.

[ELLIE *hands* HANNAH *an extra book lying around the classroom.*]

ELLIE: Mr. Von Seggern wants us to write a paragraph. One paragraph. Just one . . . about a place in nature where we like to go to get away and think. Describe it and explain how you feel being there. Why it is so special.

EVAN, HANNAH, ROBERT: He wants us to write a whole paragraph???????

ELLIE: Yes, about a place in nature. Anywhere. The beach, your backyard, a park . . . where we go to think. Tell him why we like it.

EVAN: That's too much work!

ROBERT: No way we are getting that done by tomorrow!

HANNAH: My hands are tired!

ELLIE: Then I guess I won't be in your group anymore. I quit.

[ELLIE *starts to leave.*]

HANNAH: You can't do that. We need you, Ellie. [HANNAH *goes over and hugs* ELLIE.] You've always been there for me. Every time I ran away I knew I could call you and you would listen to me, meet me at the bus stop, and take me home to wherever I was staying that week!

ROBERT: You really care about people!

EVAN: Remember that time when my cousin got shot and killed? You gave me a lollipop and told me not to cry because I still had four more cousins left.

ELLIE: Yes . . . we sure had good times together. All right, I'll stay on the condition that you write that paragraph . . . RIGHT NOW.

HANNAH: Yeah . . . sure . . . of course . . . we can do that.

[*They sit and write it quickly.*]

EVAN: Here's mine. The Tree, by Evan. "When I go out to my backyard, I sit by the tree where my cat is buried. The cat that was killed by Sushi's brother. His name was Toby. I think of Toby and lean against the tree. The tree is a place of rest. The tree is Toby's headstone. It reminds me that life can be over at any minute."

ELLIE: Good job, Evan.

HANNAH: I'm done. The Beach, by Hannah. "I like the beach. It's amazing. I like to make out there with my boyfriend. Maybe that is not so hot. But, when I listen to the waves, I kind of like, feel very good inside. Like I don't have any problems. There is meaning to everything."

ELLIE: Nice. Thoreau would be proud.

ROBERT: You gotta hear mine! Nature Sucks! by Robert. "Nature sucks. I hate it. I hate leaves and trees. I hate to pick up dog crap in my yard. But I like rocks. I can throw them at people. I wish I was a rock, so I wouldn't have to feel any pain."

ELLIE: Wow Robert . . . you wrote more than one sentence. I'm impressed.

ROBERT: We rock, Ellie! Don't we?

ELLIE: Yes, we definitely do. Well, it seems we're set for tomorrow. Give me your papers so you don't lose them.

[*They all go and hug her and give her the papers.*]

ROBERT: Wait a minute. What about yours?

HANNAH: Yeah.

EVAN: Yeah.

ELLIE: [*Reading her paper.*] I Go to Nature, by Ellie. "I sit in the woods and think of all the creatures in this world big and small. The strong and the weak, the straight and the twisted, the beautiful and the cursed . . . and know they all need nurturance and love, shelter from the elements, nutrients to feed on, a sky to gaze upon, and if injured, a second chance. I see a baby bird that has fallen from its nest. With a leaf I place drops of water in its beak. It feels good to be a small part of that second chance."

[*Beat.*]

ALL: We're getting an A for sure!

[*They all high-five.*]

Amalia's Woodland Adventure

Cassandra Lewis

Dramatic

AMALIA: 10

ELWOOD THE TREE: any age

AMALIA *is 10 years old. She's taking her puppy for a walk by herself for the first time. He runs into the forest when she lets him wander without a leash. She decides to venture into the forest after him and meets a talking tree.*

AMALIA: Bandit! Bandit! Where are you?

ELWOOD THE TREE: You should have kept him on a leash.

AMALIA: Who said that?

ELWOOD THE TREE: I did.

[AMALIA *looks around but doesn't notice the tree.*]

ELWOOD THE TREE: Over here. I don't see how you can miss me. I'm one of the biggest trees in the forest.

AMALIA: A talking tree?

ELWOOD THE TREE: Yes, of course. Why shouldn't trees talk? We drink water, create oxygen for people and animals to breathe, and provide food and shelter to wildlife.

AMALIA: Sorry. I didn't know.

ELWOOD THE TREE: You thought we were just here for decoration or to hold up your swing.

AMALIA: I know that wood from trees makes up a lot of things, like my house, our furniture, the paper I use for homework and art, and the books I read.

ELWOOD THE TREE: But you never bothered to think about our purpose before we're cut down to make things. It's okay, it's not your fault. Kids your age don't spend as much time outdoors as they used to. You're too busy playing video games and watching TV.

AMALIA: I take walks in the forest all the time. But usually I go with my mom or dad. This is my first time walking Bandit by myself. Have you seen him? He's a small black and white puppy.

ELWOOD THE TREE: Ah yes, Bandit the puppy. Short hair with a large pink tongue and a drooling problem? Yes, I've seen him. He's quite fast, even though he's still learning how to run with those big feet of his that he hasn't grown into yet. It must be like when you try on a pair of your mother's shoes and try to walk in them.

AMALIA: Did you see which way he went?

ELWOOD THE TREE: [*Pointing.*] He went that way. Into the forest.

AMALIA: Oh no!

ELWOOD THE TREE: Relax. He'll come back. You should go back inside and tell your parents.

AMALIA: No, I can't. This is my first time taking him on a walk by myself. If I go back inside without him, they'll never let me walk him again.

ELWOOD THE TREE: Well, you can't go into the forest by yourself.

AMALIA: Why not?

ELWOOD THE TREE: It's not safe. You don't know your way around.

AMALIA: How hard can it be?

ELWOOD THE TREE: The forest is vast and full of interesting characters. Some may be helpful and others may deliberately mislead you. How will you be able to know the difference? Besides, it will be dark soon.

AMALIA: I'm almost ten. I've been hiking and camping and I even know how to swim. I'll be fine.

ELWOOD THE TREE: No, Amalia, I'm telling you. You shouldn't venture into the forest by yourself.

AMALIA: How do you know my name?

ELWOOD THE TREE: I know everything.

AMALIA: Oh, yeah. What's the capital of Ethiopia?

ELWOOD THE TREE: Addis Ababa.

AMALIA: How many keys are on a piano?

ELWOOD THE TREE: Eighty-eight.

AMALIA: That's impressive. How about something more personal? What is my favorite food?

ELWOOD THE TREE: That's easy. Succotash.

AMALIA: Wow. You really do know everything.

ELWOOD THE TREE: Everyone knows that's your favorite food, Amalia. Most people ask more challenging questions, like how to achieve world peace.

AMALIA: Okay, if you're so smart. Where exactly is my puppy?

ELWOOD THE TREE: In the forest, not far from Naaman's Creek. Right now he's chatting with Boris the Beaver. He's telling him some silly jokes that he stole from some Popsicle sticks, like, Why did the policeman arrest the baseball player?

AMALIA: Why?

ELWOOD THE TREE: He stole second base. And, how does thread get to school?

AMALIA: How?

ELWOOD THE TREE: A spool bus.

AMALIA: Those aren't very funny.

ELWOOD THE TREE: Well, your puppy thinks they're hilarious. I guess he's still developing his sense of humor.

See, Bandit seems to be making friends. He'll be fine and he'll come home when he starts getting hungry. But next time, you really should put him on a leash.

AMALIA: You know why I didn't put him on a leash? I wanted to teach him how to follow instructions. He already learned his name, so I figured the next step would be to teach him to come back to me when I call his name. Everyone makes mistakes when they're learning. That's how we remember how to do it correctly the next time. That's how we learn. If I didn't give him the chance to try, then he'd never learn anything. And if you don't learn, you just end up doing the same boring things over and over. Who wants that?

People are like this too, you know. My grandfather didn't speak a word of English or know anyone when he moved here as a teenager. It was summertime and especially hot. He just stayed at home with his mother, my great-grandmother, afraid to go anywhere because he thought people would make fun of him for being different.

She offered to take him to the pool so he could cool off and meet other kids. He said no. She offered to send him to summer camp where he would learn interesting things about nature and science. But again he said no. All summer he did nothing but stay inside and worry about all the mean things the kids might say to him when he started at school in the fall. He missed an entire summer because all he could do was worry.

Then September came and it was time to start school. He felt sick to his stomach and told his mother he didn't want to go. She almost let him stay home, but then she wondered when it would end. She thought, if I let him stay home one day then he'll want to stay home another and soon he'll never start school and he'll just sit around doing nothing but worry just like he did all summer. So she took his temperature, just to make sure he wasn't really sick, and when she saw that he had no fever, she made him go to school. He begged her to let him stay, but she insisted he go.

He was terrified. But when he got on the bus the other kids smiled and said hello. He said hello back and got to school without anything terrible happening. That wasn't so bad, he thought. It's not even eight o'clock and I've already learned how to take the bus. When the bus arrived at school, a teacher welcomed him and walked him to the classroom and showed him where to sit and introduced him to another student who would be his buddy and help him learn his way around. After the first bell rang, the teacher started class by asking everyone, the whole class, to introduce themselves. When it got to my grandfather's turn, he realized that this was the first day of school for everyone, not just him, and he realized that the other kids may have been just as nervous as he was. And knowing this made him relax. He realized that each one of us is unique, and even though we are coming from different circumstances, we are all learning something that is new to us. We have this in common.

So, yes, I am walking the dog by myself for the first time and he has run away into the forest. I made a mistake and he made a mistake and we're both learning from it. But I bet the next time we go for a walk, it will be a different experience than it is today.

ELWOOD THE TREE: Yes, I'm sure it will be. I'll tell him to hurry back to you if he passes this way again.

AMALIA: Which way did you say he went?

ELWOOD THE TREE: [*Pointing.*] That way. But you'd better not go after him.

AMALIA: I'll be fine, especially now that I've been warned about Boris the Beaver and his Popsicle stick jokes.

ELWOOD THE TREE: If you insist on going, stay on the trail beside the creek and turn back before the sun sets. If you start noticing fireflies, then it's time to turn around and head home. Whatever you do don't follow the fireflies. All they do is dance. They're a lot of fun, but they won't be able to help you find your way home. If anything, they'll lead you deeper into the forest.

AMALIA: Thanks. What did you say your name was?

ELWOOD THE TREE: Elwood. Elwood the Tree. I know everyone in the forest, so if you run into trouble, just let it be known that you're a friend of mine. In the meantime, I'll try to spread the word that you're on your way.

AMALIA: Thanks, Elwood. See you again soon.

[AMALIA *ventures into the forest.*]

Annie Jump and the Library of Heaven

Reina Hardy

Seriocomic

KJ: 14
ANNIE: 13

KJ *enters, holding a flashlight.*

KJ: Pete—yo, P.T.! Can you even believe this shiz? I almost peed. Pete? Where are you?

[ANNIE, *wearing a hard hat with a light on it, stands up, seemingly out of nowhere. She's been fiddling with some electronics.*]

KJ: Who are you?

ANNIE: I'm the electrician.

KJ: Aren't you a girl?

ANNIE: Excuse me?

KJ: No, I mean . . .

ANNIE: What are you, twelve?

KJ: I'm a sophomore in high school. I'm a little short for my age but it's temporary. I haven't grown into my feet yet.

ANNIE: Oh. I'm a freshman.

KJ: Also I skipped a grade.

ANNIE: Me too. [*She hunkers down and gets back to work.*] I've never seen you before.

KJ: I'm new in town this summer.

ANNIE: And you're hanging out with Pete and those guys?

KJ: We were pranking somebody. I'm, kind of like a tech guy—so my contribution was pretty crucial to the success of the project.

ANNIE: What did you do?

KJ: I sent a fax to Christopher Jump.

ANNIE: Oh yeah. Dr. Alien.

KJ: I guess he's like, a legend in this town. Has this crazy website asking for e-mails from little green men, and everyone laughs at him but he's just like, whatever, "I Believe." Is he actually a doctor?

ANNIE: He has a doctorate. Psychology.

KJ: Whoah. Legit? That's amazing. 'Cause he's, y'know . . .

ANNIE: Crazy?

KJ: Yeah. So did you hear the name of the alien federation? Association of Stellar Serenity Healing Across Time Space.

[Annie *thinks for a second.*]

ANNIE: Asshats?

[KJ *cracks up.*]

KJ: I can't believe he didn't notice! I still gotta think of the perfect song for Dr. Jump to sing to the aliens.

ANNIE: How about the Barney song? Y'know—I love you, you love me, we're a happy . . .

KJ: Happy family? OMG, that's perfect. You're a genius.

ANNIE: Uh-huh.

KJ: So, you're from around here? You're like, a Strawberry?

ANNIE: I guess so. Can you do me a favor and make sure this is grounded?

KJ: Eh. Uh. I'm not really good with wiring.

ANNIE: I thought you said you were a tech guy?

KJ: More computers. Programming, software, that kind of thing. But I can try to . . .

ANNIE: Don't stress. I've got it.

[KJ *shines his flashlight on* ANNIE *for a second.*]

KJ: This is so weird.

ANNIE: Hmm?

KJ: You are definitely a girl, but . . .

ANNIE: What?

KJ: Nothing. You're just surprising, that's all.

ANNIE: Surprising in a good way, or a bad way?

KJ: Good way. Definitely a good way.

ANNIE: What's your name?

KJ: Oh, shiz. I totally forgot. I'm not nonfunctional or anything, just a little weird sometimes. I'm Kenneth Jerome Urbanik. My friends call me KJ. What's your name?

[ANNIE *stands.*]

ANNIE: I'm Annie. Annie Jump.

Annie Jump and the Library of Heaven

Reina Hardy

Seriocomic

ANNIE: 13
ALTHEA: 13 to 15

ANNIE *is sitting outside, looking at the stars. A small, round object drops out of the sky and rolls to her feet. She picks it up. It's a pool ball. The eight.*

ANNIE: . . . the heck?

ALTHEA: That's mine, you know.

[*A very pretty, nicely dressed teenage girl with a good deal of attitude has appeared.*]

ANNIE: What?

ALTHEA: That thing you just picked up. It belongs to me.

ANNIE: Um . . .

ALTHEA: Do you understand American English? It's mine.

ANNIE: It came from the sky. [ALTHEA *gives her a look.* ANNIE *withers.*] Do you want it back?

ALTHEA: I just wanted you to know it was mine. [ALTHEA *goes and sits on a rock and begins brushing her hair. Her hair is totally beautiful.*]

ANNIE: Who are you?

ALTHEA: You can call me Althea.

ANNIE: Is that your real name or just something you made up?

ALTHEA: Do you think I would just go around making up a name like Althea?

ANNIE: What are you, an oil kid?

ALTHEA: An oil kid?

ANNIE: The rich kids always have superfancy names. Clementine. Dashiell. Are you new?

ALTHEA: I just got here.

ANNIE: Well, look. I'm sorry to mess up your plans for tonight, but this is my rock. And I have plans of my own. So can you just text whoever it is and tell him to meet you somewhere else?

ALTHEA: Meet who where?

ANNIE: Y'know, Pete Stockholm, or Darcy, or whichever boy you're planning to make out with. . . . Oh come on. Don't pretend you're out here to watch the Perseids.

ALTHEA: The Perseids?

ANNIE: It's a meteor shower visible from Earth that comes around once every August—they call it that because it looks like they're all coming from the constellation Perseus but that's just an illusion caused by . . .

ALTHEA: I know what the Perseids are.

ANNIE: Sure you do.

ALTHEA: I know everything you know.

ANNIE: You don't have to be embarrassed. I don't judge. We all have our areas of expertise. Mine is engineering and astronomy. Yours is. I don't know. Hair. Shoes. Boys. I mean, someone has to do it, I guess. Just . . . not on my stargazing rock, okay?

ALTHEA: I didn't come here to make out with some smelly teenage boy.

ANNIE: So you did come here for the Perseids.

ALTHEA: I came here for you, Annie Jump.

ANNIE: Whoah. How do you know my name? What did you do—look through the middle-school yearbook?

ALTHEA: Seriously?

ANNIE: You threw a pool ball at me. Are you some kind of lesbian?

ALTHEA: [*Thinks about the question for a second.*] No. I'm the visual manifestation of a mindful of an intergalactic computer built and maintained by a collection of the most advanced intelligent species in the universe. [*Beat.*]

ANNIE: You know what? Screw you. You are a terrible human being.

ALTHEA: I just told you that I'm not a human being.

ANNIE: It's not my fault, okay? It's my dad. I didn't ask for him. I don't encourage him. I would like it if he just shut up and went away also, all right? But he won't. He never will, and I have to deal with that my whole life, so you don't have to rub my face in it. I came out here to be *alone*. I came out here to watch a *meteor shower*. I didn't come out here to get made fun of by some popular fluffhead for something that I didn't even do.

ALTHEA: What makes you think I'm popular? Is it more the clothes, or is it the hair? I'm very proud of the hair.

ANNIE: Sometimes I wish I were pretty.

ALTHEA: Why would you wish that?

ANNIE: Because when you're pretty, you can be as weird as you like, and no one even notices.

ALTHEA: You're only three-eighths as smart as you think you are, Annie Jump.

ANNIE: That's rich, considering the source.

ALTHEA: That source being a manifestation of a mindfurl of an intergalactic super computer. I told you, Annie, I know everything you know, and everything you don't know, and everything you're not allowed to know. I pretty much know everything.

ANNIE: Yeah, right.

ALTHEA: Try me.

ANNIE: I'm not as dumb as my father is.

ALTHEA: Try. Me.

ANNIE: Okay. Who discovered Cepheid variable stars?

ALTHEA: Henrietta Swan Leavvit, the Harvard computer.

ANNIE: What's Kepler's third law of planetary motion?

ALTHEA: The square of the orbital period of a planet is proportional to the cube of the semimajor axis of its orbit. Come on, Annie. This is high school stuff!

ANNIE: Fine. What's the initial step in Wile's proof of Fermat's last theorem?

ALTHEA: Given an elliptic curve E over the field Q of rational numbers, for every prime power there exists a homomorphism from the absolute Galois group. [*Beat.*]

ANNIE: Crap!

ALTHEA: I told you. I know everything.

ANNIE: How do you reconcile quantum mechanics with general relativity?

ALTHEA: I can't tell you that.

ANNIE: Too complex for you?

ALTHEA: It's too complex for *you*. But the real reason I can't tell you is that there's a slight chance you'll understand it. I'm not supposed to reveal any truths or any information not currently known on planet Earth. No telling you the answers to the big questions, no giving you alien technologies. It's kind of like my prime directive.

ANNIE: No big questions, huh?

ALTHEA: Well, I can give you one. Are we alone in the universe? Hint hint. You're not.

ANNIE: What are you even doing out here?

ALTHEA: I told you. I'm here for you. I know everything about everything. But I also know everything about you, Annie.

ANNIE: That's creepy.

ALTHEA: I know what happened to your mom when you were little. I know about your dad. I know your Gmail password.

ANNIE: No.

ALTHEA: Stardate 403604. I know your middle-school grade in intermediate Spanish. A-minus.

ANNIE: Stop it.

ELWOOD THE TREE: I know your father used to read to you from *A Wrinkle in Time*. I know your grandparents sued him for custody when you were three and again when you were five, and again when you were seven. I know you were a muppet for your eighth Halloween party, yip yip yip yip yip yip yip . . .

ANNIE: You're a total freak.

ALTHEA: I know you wrote Carl Sagan a fan e-mail when you saw his television show and thought he was alive. I can list all of your father's court-ordered prescription meds. I know the only solo you ever sang in grade school choir: [*She sings.*] "Somewhere out there, beneath the pale moonlight . . ."

ANNIE: [*Overlapping with song.*] Stop it! Just stop it—go away! Go away!

ALTHEA: You can't get rid of me, Annie. You're the one. You're the Chosen One.

[*Beat.* ANNIE *runs offstage.*]

As It Is in Heaven

Arlene Hutton

Dramatic

IZZY: 10 to 15; she is the youngest of the three and was orphaned as a baby.

FANNY: 10 to 15; she is escaping an abusive home situation.

POLLY: 10 to 15; she previously worked at a "fancy house" in Louisville before being rescued.

The setting is 1838 and takes place at Pleasant Hill, a Shaker community in Kentucky. IZZY, orphaned as a baby, has been raised by the Shaker sisters and is the youngest of the three friends. POLLY was working at a "fancy house" in Louisville when she was rescued and brought to the village. FANNY, a newcomer escaping an abusive home situation, wants to fit in with the community but is trying to understand the spiritual manifestations she is experiencing. The scene is outdoors, near the village. IZZY sees FANNY, who keeps moving around the stage as if she were walking on a trail through the woods, stepping over imaginary rocks and logs and crossing a small stream.

IZZY: Fanny! [*No answer.* IZZY *follows* FANNY.] Fanny! [IZZY *catches up to* FANNY. FANNY *walks a while,* IZZY *behind.*]

FANNY: Don't you have chores?

IZZY: Finished. Fed the chickens. I can come with you.

FANNY: I don't recollect inviting you.

IZZY: I want to see . . . see the . . .

[FANNY *turns to face* IZZY.]

FANNY: See what? What is it you want to see?

IZZY: What you've been seeing.

FANNY: I've been seeing blueberries. And I aim to pick us some. Gonna spoil that nice white apron o'yours if you come pickin' blueberries with me.

[IZZY *turns to go as* POLLY *runs on stage.*]

POLLY: [*To* FANNY.] Was looking for you.

FANNY: Getting to be a party now, Polly.

IZZY: [*To* POLLY.] Fanny's going to pick blueberries.

POLLY: Too early for blueberries.

FANNY: Found some early ones.

IZZY: Early ones'll be sour.

POLLY: She's going out past the meadow.

IZZY: [*To* FANNY.] You said you were going berry picking.

POLLY: Where's her pail, then?

IZZY: You don't have a pail!

[*Beat.*]

FANNY: Just wanted to be alone. Not used to spending every waking minute someone by my side. Just like to go sit and look at the trees sometimes.

IZZY: I won't bother you. I won't even talk to you.

POLLY: You're seeing something in the trees.

FANNY: [*Starting to leave.*] Sure, I am. Birds. I'm seeing birds in the trees. And squirrels.

[POLLY *is following* FANNY *throughout the following dialogue.* IZZY *tags along.*]

IZZY: Are there baby squirrels? Funny how you never see baby squirrels. Baby birds. You see them. Once I found a baby bird fallen out of its nest. I put it back.

POLLY: It died.

IZZY: How do you know? I put it back.

POLLY: Mama bird won't touch a young'un after a person's handled it.

IZZY: Maybe it didn't die.

POLLY: Won't touch it once it's tainted with a human smell. Momma bird won't have anything t'do with it.

FANNY: You saved it, Izzy. You saved its life.

[*They keep walking.*]

IZZY: Once I found a hummingbird caught in a spider web. I pulled that spider web oft it. Flew off, happy as could be. Aren't hummingbirds the most beautiful thing? Little spirits flying around. Little angels, almost.

POLLY: Fanny sees angels. You told me you did. Unless it was a false gift.

FANNY: Weren't false. Ain't no false gift.

POLLY: If you're seeing something, then show us. I think it's a lying gift. I don't believe in spirits and angels nohow.

IZZY: Mother Ann saw spirits.

POLLY: She's making it up. She's lying.

[FANNY *stops and stares westward.*]

IZZY: [*To* FANNY.] Are you making it up?

POLLY: She's making it up. I'm going back. I'm hungry.

FANNY: There's berries over there.

POLLY: Too early for berries.

[IZZY *sees the berries.*]

IZZY: Those are the biggest blueberries I ever saw. Don't see any squirrels or birds. Sure is quiet here.

POLLY: There it is!

[POLLY *"gooses"* IZZY, *who squeals.*]

IZZY: Where?

POLLY: Sun's about to set. There's nothing here.

FANNY: Over there.

POLLY: Where?

FANNY: There.

[FANNY *points.*]

IZZY: Where?

POLLY: An angel?

FANNY: Don't know.

IZZY: I should be getting back.

POLLY: You scared?

FANNY: Thought you wanted to see.

IZZY: I do.

[FANNY *suddenly stops.*]

FANNY: Then look.

IZZY: Don't see anything. Where am I supposed to look?

POLLY: It's getting warmer. Should be getting cooler, but it's getting warmer.

FANNY: Hush.

POLLY: What do you see?

FANNY: Hush.

IZZY: I'm scared.

FANNY: [*Whispering.*] Don't be scared, Izzy. It's the most beautiful thing you ever did see.

IZZY: [*Whispering back.*] More beautiful than a hummingbird?

FANNY: Like a hundred hummingbirds all at once.

[FANNY *holds out her arms.*]

IZZY: Ohhhh. [FANNY *closes her eyes.* IZZY *and* POLLY *look skyward.*] Ohhh, I see light.

FANNY: Hush.

POLLY: Where? [FANNY *stands and faces the light as if it were sunlight streaming on her face after a long dark winter.*] What do you see?

IZZY: So beautiful!

POLLY: Don't see anything except the pink clouds!

IZZY: The light!

POLLY: It's the sunset, silly.

IZZY: I hear the wings! Like a hundred hummingbirds! Oh, oh, oh . . .

POLLY: Just the breeze, Izzy. Just a warm breeze rustling though the trees.

[POLLY *shakes* IZZY, *who continues to look all around.*]

IZZY: Gold. All gold.

POLLY: Where?

FANNY: What do you hear, Izzy?

IZZY: Music? Singing? Sounds like I never heard before.

POLLY: [*Shouting.*] You're making it up! It's just a sunset.

FANNY: Look at the clouds, Polly.

POLLY: You're making it up!

FANNY: Look at the clouds!

POLLY: [*Covering her face.*] No.

FANNY: Does that look like any sunset you've ever seen before?

POLLY: [*In denial.*] No.

IZZY: Like a thousand hummingbirds!

[IZZY *and* FANNY *run off.* POLLY *runs in the opposite direction.*]

Augusta and Noble

Carlos Murillo

Dramatic

RICARDO: 13
GABI: 13

Afternoon. A grassy lot with a view of the Chicago skyline.
RICARDO appears with his backpack. GABI has been kicking a
soccer ball around with her brother, Jesus, but he's left. In this,
the final scene of the play, GABI tells RICARDO the true story of
her origins and her parents' harrowing immigration to America.

RICARDO: Hey.

GABI: Hey . . .

RICARDO: So . . . this is the place?

GABI: Yeah. Do you like it?

RICARDO: When you said "park," I thought you meant
like a *park* . . .

GABI: It *is* a park.

RICARDO: Well, it's really an empty lot.

GABI: It's got grass. It's got this view . . . You could sit down . . .

[*He sits.*]

RICARDO: Definitely a nice view. I've never been to this neighborhood before.

GABI: I come here when I want to just sit and think.

RICARDO: What do you think about?

GABI: How beautiful the city is. What it was like for my mother and father seeing all the buildings for the first time.

RICARDO: There aren't buildings where they come from?

GABI: Not like these. I like this place 'cause it feels like you can reach out and touch them.

RICARDO: They seem like a million miles away to me.

GABI: Ever feel like you've got your feet in two different worlds? And you feel like you're getting split down the middle?

RICARDO: All the time. . . . My mom? She gets mad at me if I act too "Polish." My dad, he gets mad if I act too "Puerto Rican."

GABI: What does that mean?

RICARDO: I have no idea . . . I'm just trying to figure out who I'm supposed to be, which gets them both mad 'cause then I'm being too American. [*Pause.*] I'm glad you called . . . I thought you were still mad.

GABI: I'm not mad. It was hard, but it helped me ask questions that . . .

RICARDO: That . . . ?

GABI: I was too scared to ask before?

RICARDO: What kind of questions?

[*She looks at him seriously.*]

GABI: Can I trust you?

[RICARDO *thinks for a moment—no one has ever asked him that with as much seriousness as* GABI *is asking him now.*]

RICARDO: Yeah . . .

[GABI *looks back at the skyline. She takes a deep breath, like she's about to jump off the high dive for the first time.*]

GABI: I was born here. But my parents? They were born in Mexico . . .

RICARDO: Okay . . .

GABI: They've been here a long time, but . . . They're not really . . . supposed . . . to be here.

RICARDO: You mean . . .

GABI: They're here illegally.

RICARDO: Whoa.

GABI: They walked all the way across the desert to come.

RICARDO: That's terrifying.

GABI: They wanted a better life. For me. For Jesus. My father, he had to go back. To see his father before he died. Now he's coming home. He has to cross the desert again.

RICARDO: That's really scary, Gabi.

GABI: If he gets caught? They could send him back . . . My mother too . . .

RICARDO: What would happen to you?

GABI: I don't know. Guess I would have to go back with them.

RICARDO: But you belong here . . .

[GABI *looks at him.*]

GABI: I do?

RICARDO: You do.

[*Pause.* GABI *looks at him.*]

GABI: I don't know what's going to happen, Ricardo. But . . . One thing I want to do . . . ?

Finish Ms. Chan's project. Find out the incredible history we have inside of us. I want to do it right this time.

RICARDO: You mean as like . . . partners?

GABI: Yes, Ricardo.

RICARDO: Cool . . . I'd . . . like that. So . . . when do we like . . . start?

GABI: Well, it's Saturday. We can go to my house. Interview my mom. She doesn't have work tonight. She's making dinner. You can try some real Mexican food.

RICARDO: I've eaten Mexican before . . .

GABI: No, I mean like *real* Mexican, the way my mom makes it . . .

RICARDO: Maybe tomorrow you can come to my mom's? Only place in the city where you can eat some authentic Polish-Puerto Rican . . .

[*They laugh.*]

GABI: Um . . . Ricardo . . . ? Just so you know, like . . . I'm inviting you to my house as like . . . you know . . . a friend?

RICARDO: Oh, yeah, sure—I'm not sure I'm really into girls, so . . . ooops.

GABI: I see . . .

RICARDO: Does that . . . ?

GABI: Doesn't bother me.

RICARDO: Cool . . . um. Shall we go?

GABI: Meet me up at the corner of Augusta and Noble— I'll be there in a second.

Bad Ideas for
Terrible Things

Gabrielle Sinclair

Seriocomic

KEL: 11 to 14
JENNY: 11 to 14

After receiving a frantic phone call, KEL *meets her best friend* JENNY *to track down the mysterious ghost that is rumored to inhabit an old abandoned house.*

KEL: What?

JENNY: Nothing.

[*Pause.*]

JENNY: It's not that you have to wear pants—you just probably should wear pants . . . that's all I'm saying.

KEL: Why?

JENNY: Because!

KEL: I'm not tucking my freakin' pants into my socks. I'll look like an idiot.

[*Pause.*]

JENNY: Who said anything about socks?

KEL: This should be a simple thing.

JENNY: You can borrow my pants. I have so many pants.

[KEL *points up to the house.*]

KEL: There isn't a *bee* up there, Jenny. It's not a swarm of *bees.*

JENNY: I'm aware it's not a swarm of bees.

KEL: Do you not like this skirt?

JENNY: It doesn't matter. It's a skirt.

KEL: The ghost in the crawl space isn't going to *fly up my skirt*, Jenny!

JENNY: Shh!

KEL: What.

JENNY: He'll hear you.

KEL: It's a he?

JENNY: Maybe. He seems like a he. Aloof. Confusing. Hard to read.

KEL: So just to be clear. You believe the thing in the crawl space . . .

JENNY: He's a ghost.

KEL: The ghost in the crawl space.

JENNY: Why are you calling it a crawl space?

KEL: The man ghost in the attic is a creep who is going to sneak up my skirt.

JENNY: I just don't want you to be embarrassed.

KEL: Don't ghosts walk through walls?

JENNY: I don't know. I don't know anything.

[*Silence.*]

KEL: You're being really weird about this skirt, and I just got it. And it's cute. And it doesn't belong to you.

JENNY: It just seems weird. Why do you have to dress up like you're going to prom for everything?

KEL: Really?

JENNY: It's just like—it's not a joke, ya know?

KEL: What does that mean?

JENNY: And it's not like—it's not like—this isn't like on the way to something. Meeting a ghost isn't on the way to something. Ya know?

KEL: I don't even . . .

JENNY: I mean—did you make plans? Are you going to a movie? Do you have a movie you have to be at?

KEL: Jesus Christ.

JENNY: What?

KEL: Ya know, people *die* in crawl spaces.

JENNY: It's an attic.

KEL: It's a crawl space. And it's old. And rickety and full of tics and splinters and tetanus and *maybe* a ghost. I might fall through. Accidentally stab myself. I might be *eaten by a ghost*. But I am here, aren't I? I'm here—right? I showed up. You called me, freaking out that we *have* to do this, and I am here. And I might die. And guess what—I really like this skirt—it's flattering but not overly you know—cute without being child-like—it's comfortable without being tomboyish—it's like everything I always wanted in a skirt—If I'm gonna die at 4:30 in the afternoon with you, I wanna be wearing this skirt, all right?!

[*Silence.*]

JENNY: I wish this was fun.

[*Silence.*]

KEL: So you don't actually think that ghost is a creep.

JENNY: No, I think he's probably one of the greatest people who ever was alive once. I think he's probably super nice and lonely and kind. I think he's gonna have lots to share about history and—ya know—things to not repeat— like lessons. Lessons. About mistakes! I bet no one ever asks him about himself because they're thinking about running away from him or about their skirts.

[*Silence.* KEL *sees* JENNY *is upset. She takes a step toward her.*]

KEL: I bet it sucks being stuck up there.

JENNY: It sucks being stuck anywhere.

[*Pause.*]

KEL: Maybe we could help him move out into the backyard or something.

[*A moment.* JENNY *brightens.*]

JENNY: Yeah! Definitely. Maybe—Or at least into the living room.

KEL: That would be so great.

[*A moment.* JENNY *reaches her hand up to the door. She looks to* KEL, *who nods.* JENNY *knocks on the door three times, loudly. They wait.* JENNY *grins.*]

JENNY: Here we go.

KEL: Here we go.

[JENNY *pushes open the door. They enter. The door closes behind them.*]

Booty

Steven Schutzman

Comic

EDDIE: 8
STAR: 8

Both girls are African American.

EDDIE *is sitting on a stoop, playing jacks on the landing.* STAR *saunters in vamping and preening like an innocent 8-year-old might imitate a sexy, grown-up woman.*

EDDIE: [*Shaking her head.*] Hey, Star.

STAR: Hello, Edwina.

EDDIE: Edwina?

STAR: And you can call me Starchella from now on.

EDDIE: Get over yourself, girl.

STAR: Ha!

EDDIE: Ha! [*Pause.*] Let's play.

STAR: I don't think so.

EDDIE: Why not? I been waitin' for you. Like forever.

STAR: It's childish.

EDDIE: It's childish. We're children, last time I looked.

STAR: Not anymore. I got me a nice booty.

EDDIE: What?

STAR: A nice, bodacious booty.

EDDIE: [*Getting down to look at* STAR's *feet.*] Nikes ain't booties, girl; they're sneaks, and nasty. Not nice. Just nasty.

STAR: I'm not talkin' 'bout boots, stupid. I'm talkin' 'bout booty.

EDDIE: Where?

STAR: My booty is up and down and all over me.

EDDIE: Where at?

STAR: Wherever a boy's eyes go on me, that's where my booty is.

EDDIE: Nasty.

STAR: Says you.

EDDIE: Says me is right.

STAR: Ha!

EDDIE: Ha! Okay. What's a booty?

STAR: You don't know?

EDDIE: Nope, just that it sound nasty.

STAR: Well then, I'm not tellin' you.

EDDIE: Hey, you don't know either.

STAR: Maybe not, maybe not, Edwina, but Jaden just told me I got me a nice, bodacious one.

EDDIE: Jaden! In fourth grade? That boy always tryin' to hang with them teenagers on the corner? Up on his bike, runnin' to the store for them and such?

STAR: That's right. [*She waves toward a distant corner.*] Hey, Jaden!

EDDIE: [*Shaking her head.*] Stop it. Now, do you wanna play now or what, Starchella?

STAR: No, I do not, Eddie.

EDDIE: Well, that Jaden's a dunce.

STAR: I don't think so.

EDDIE: With that stupid grin of his. A definite dunce.

STAR: I do not think so. [*Beat.*] Okay. What's a dunce?

EDDIE: You don't know dunce and you don't know booty.

STAR: Okay, but what is it?

EDDIE: I don't know either, exactly. Sounds real bad though. My grandpa always be sayin' to my father like when he comes home all red-eyed and raggedy, "When you gonna stop being such a damn fool dunce, Elmore?"

My father say, shakin' his head, "I don't know, Daddy," all red-eyed and sorry like. So it can't be good.

STAR: Who cares? Jaden practically a man.

EDDIE: Him? Ha!

STAR: He be tall and he be lookin' your booty up and down like a man.

EDDIE: He be nine.

STAR: [*She waves again.*] Hey, Jaden!

EDDIE: Stop it. Or he'll come over here and ruin the game.

STAR: So what?

EDDIE: He prob'ly don't know what a booty is either.

STAR: Sure act like he do.

EDDIE: So?

STAR: Like he's a man and I'm a woman.

EDDIE: Nasty.

STAR: Up and down and all over my body. [*Looking down and discovering her body is the same as it ever was. Beat. More innocent now.*] Anyway, them teenagers might'a told him what it is.

EDDIE: I guess. But who cares?

STAR: You prob'ly got you a nice booty too, since we're best friends.

EDDIE: I doubt it.

STAR: Well, then, we could share mine. Since we best friends.

EDDIE: Whatever. Let's play.

STAR: We can get Jaden over here. He look us up one side and down the other, with eyes all big like this . . .

EDDIE: No!

STAR: He look you front and back, all grinning like this . . .

EDDIE: No!

STAR: And he say, Nice booty, Mama.

EDDIE: Mama?

STAR: Nice bodacious booty, Mama. [*Pause.*] I'll just call Jaden over. Hey, Jaden . . . [*She waves.*]

EDDIE: [*Stopping her.*] Stop it, Star. Stop it. I mean it. I don't want that boy over here, now or ever.

STAR: You just jealous 'cause I got me such a nice booty.

EDDIE: No way. I just don't want that boy sayin' nothin' 'bout my booty. I don't want him lookin' and grinnin'. I don't wanna know nothin' 'bout no booty, at all. It's prob'ly stupid like he is. Or he made it up. I don't want it. And I don't wanna be no Mama, workin', yellin', tired all the time. All I wanna do is play jacks like always. Now, you wanna play with me or not?

[STAR *looks over to the corner where Jaden is. She looks at* EDDIE.]

STAR: Yeah, I guess. We can play for a little while.

[*The girls play jacks.*]

Cheating

Olivia Arieti

Dramatic

PAT: 14 to 15; a teenage girl.
JOEL: 14 to 15; PAT's sister's boyfriend.

PAT *has fallen for* JOEL *but he happens to be her sister's boyfriend.* JOEL, *though, appears superficial and insensitive to* PAT's *feelings and to the problems teenage girls have to face. This scene takes place on a park bench.* JOEL *enters, looks around, sits on the bench. Takes out his cell phone, starts playing.* PAT *arrives.*

PAT: I'm a bit late. Sorry.

JOEL: [*Keeps on playing.*] Bingo! Boy, what a score.

PAT: Hey, I'm here, Joel.

JOEL: [*Without looking up.*] At last. I was about to leave.

PAT: [*Sits next to him.*] The problem was I . . . well . . . I really couldn't make up my mind.

JOEL: About what?

PAT: About coming here.

JOEL: [*Shows her the time.*] You're three minutes late.

PAT: Don't be silly.

JOEL: I'm not used to waiting. [*Beat.*]

PAT: I appreciated you asking me out but I shouldn't have accepted.

JOEL: Can't see why. I'm one of the coolest boys around here and you know it.

PAT: You're my sister's boyfriend, Joel.

JOEL: Who cares? Sally doesn't know.

PAT: It's not nice to cheat on her.

JOEL: Why all the fuss, Pat? You wouldn't be here if you really cared.

PAT: You know why I've come.

JOEL: Of course, I do. You like me.

PAT: Yeah, but I can't help thinking it's wrong, though. [*Pause.*] Do you care for me?

JOEL: Whoa! You're moving a little too fast, sweetie.

PAT: Do you love Sally?

JOEL: Have I ever said I did? [*Beat.*] Look, I just want to kiss you. I'm sure you want me to.

PAT: Can't deny it.

JOEL: [*Putting his arm around her.*] Well, what are we waiting for?

[*They are about to kiss.* PAT *moves away.*]

PAT: What should I say to her?

JOEL: Who?

PAT: Sally!

JOEL: No need to say anything.

PAT: That's called lying!

JOEL: Can't see how if you keep your mouth shut. Come on, baby, a little kiss won't harm anyone. [*Holds her in his arms.*] It never has.

PAT: [*Puts her finger on his lips.*] Wait. . . .

JOEL: [*Annoyed.*] What for?

PAT: Don't you feel a bit guilty?

JOEL: Not my fault if Sally has such a gorgeous sister. [PAT *moves away.*]

PAT: Sally trusts me. I'm sure she trusts you too.

JOEL: It's no big deal. Everyone does it. Molly cheats on Bill, Fred on Jane, the line is pretty long.

PAT: That's not a good reason for doing it. [*Pause.*] Have you ever cheated on Sally?

JOEL: [*Takes out a can.*] You're spoiling everything, Pat. [*Drinks. Beat.*]

PAT: I'm sure she thinks you love her.

JOEL: The problem is, you girls are too worried about your feelings.

PAT: We girls got some values and want to stick to them.

JOEL: Outdated.

PAT: Who said so?

JOEL: Me. They're causing you trouble.

PAT: I'm beginning to feel sorry for her. Wish she'd open her eyes.

JOEL: She did, trust me, and she liked what she saw.

PAT: You're the most conceited guy I've ever met.

[JOEL *gets up*.]

JOEL: That's it. I'm leaving. Thank goodness not all girls are like you. [*Takes her hand.*] You're very pretty and I like you a lot. When I'm through with Sally, we might even start going steady. What about that?

PAT: When you're *through*?

JOEL: I never get involved more than necessary.

PAT: Does she know that?

JOEL: Not my business.

PAT: You should play fair and tell her.

JOEL: Are you crazy? She'll dump me on the spot! It's too late to find another date for the school dance.

PAT: Is that the reason you keep on dating my sister?

JOEL: Be reasonable, it's only two days from now. I got it! Next year I'll go to the dance with you.

PAT: I'm really beginning to hate you. Dumping you would be the best thing Sally could do.

JOEL: You'll end up loving me as well.

PAT: Drop dead!

JOEL: You look beautiful when you're angry.

PAT: Go to hell! As for me, I'm leaving.

JOEL: Too bad for you. I won't give you another chance.

PAT: I didn't expect you to be so insensitive.

JOEL: Still here, baby?

PAT: I hope she'll hate you as much as I do. Sally has no idea of the monster she's dating!

JOEL: Your sister adores me.

PAT: Not for long, I'm sure. [*Pause.*] I'm going; this time for good. [*Gets up.*] I'm going to tell her about us.

JOEL: Not much to say, actually. [*Takes out his cell phone. Starts playing.*] By the way, don't forget to tell her I'll pick her up at six.

PAT: Over my dead body!

[*Exits.*]

[*Blackout.*]

Cinderella

Jack Neary

Comic

BLANCHE: 7 to 15
WHITEY: 7 to 15

This is the opening scene from the play. WHITEY *and* BLANCHE, *two doves, are in a graveyard.*

BLANCHE: This is just . . . this is . . . this is too much . . . I mean the tension . . . the tension is . . . it's just . . . the tension . . . the tension is . . . You know what I'm talkin' about here?

WHITEY: You're talking about the tension.

BLANCHE: Exactly. I'm talkin' about the tension. It's just . . . the tension is just . . . it's just . . .

WHITEY: Unbearable?

BLANCHE: Exactly. Unbearable. The tension is unbearable.

WHITEY: Blanche, you gotta relax.

BLANCHE: Relax? Is that what you said? Relax? How can I relax? Tell me that. Go ahead, Whitey, tell me. How? How can I relax? Better yet, why? Why should I relax?

WHITEY: Because you're a dove. You're the symbol of peace and tranquility.

BLANCHE: Well, right now I'm the symbol of tension and irritability. I can't relax. Not until I find out who the Prince is going to pick to be his bride!

WHITEY: It's out of your hands. There's nothing you can do about it.

BLANCHE: Oh, yeah? Is that right, smartypants? Well, there *is* something I can do about it. I can pace and whine and kvetch! That's what I can do about it!

WHITEY: You're embarrassing yourself.

BLANCHE: In front of who? You? Big deal!

WHITEY: No. In front of them.

[*Indicates audience.*]

BLANCHE: Them who?

[WHITEY *points.*]

WHITEY: Them!

[BLANCHE *looks at audience.*]

BLANCHE: Aaaah! Who are they?

WHITEY: The people who want to know why you're so tense!

BLANCHE: Oh. Well. Maybe we should tell them.

WHITEY: Maybe we should.

BLANCHE: All right. You start.

WHITEY: No. You start. It'll get your mind off your problem.

BLANCHE: I don't have a problem! The Prince has a problem. That's who has a problem! And if he doesn't do something about his problem pretty soon, I'm . . . I'm . . . Oh, the tension . . . the tension . . .

WHITEY: Tell them the story! From the beginning!

BLANCHE: Oh, all right, all right, all right! It all started right here a few months ago. This is where Whitey and I live . . .

WHITEY: Perch.

BLANCHE: Whatever! This is where we perch. And one day, we were perching . . . minding our own business . . . [*They get into perching positions.*] . . . when this sweet young girl appeared, carrying flowers to her mother's grave . . .

Dancing Doll

Monica Raymond

Comic

DOLL: 7 to 12, a girl
BOX: 7 to 12, a boy
DANCE FAIRY: 7 to 12, a girl

The scene takes place on the night before Christmas, or perhaps a birthday. The characters are a DOLL and a wrapped BOX. The DOLL tries to dance, but she can only make pathetic, spastic moves.

DOLL: Wake up! There's something wrong! [Box *yawns noisily.*] Come on—wake up! There's something wrong. I need to talk to someone or I'll burst!

BOX: Okay, okay—what is it?

DOLL: I'm supposed to be a dancing doll, but I can't dance.

BOX: Did you try?

DOLL: Yes!

BOX: That's the trouble. You shouldn't try.

DOLL: Why not?

BOX: You're a present, right?

DOLL: Yes.

BOX: A present is just supposed to be *present*. If you *try*, that makes you a FUTURE!! Hah! Hah!

DOLL: But how can I do it without trying?

BOX: Simple. You just . . .

DOLL: I know, I know—do it!

[DOLL *tries to dance. She gets all mixed up and starts going backward.*]

BOX: Forwards! Forwards! You're in reverse.

[*She tries to go forward. She fails. She falls.*]

DOLL: You are so *no help*!

BOX: You probably just need a battery. That's why I don't worry. I know they'll unwrap me and put in my battery and CAPOW! CHING! VOOM! BLAM BLAM BLAM! [*He makes amazing video-game noises.*] I'll be just fine.

DOLL: How do you know?

BOX: [*Singing.*] 'Cause I've got FAITH
Give me F-A-I
I've got FAITH
And that's the reason why
Add an H and T
And my new battery

And I'll fly—
Oh yes, I'll fly!

So no need to worry
No need to complain
Wet and dreary
Sitting out in the rain
I'm high and dry
With my F-A-I-
[T-H]
With my F-A-I!

DOLL: But what if they put in a battery and I *still* can't dance?

BOX: Mmm. That would be bad. You might get returned.

DOLL: Returned?

BOX: Yup. Sent back to the store.

DOLL: And then, would they fix me?

BOX: What do you think? [*Muttering to himself.*] Oh yeah, they'll fix you, all right. [*He falls asleep, snores.*]

DOLL: Oh box—oh game, oh whatever you are in your beautiful wrapping paper. I don't want to be returned. I hated that store—always having to look pretty and smile so that someone would buy you. And all the other dolls giving their fake smiley-smiles, too.

[*A twinkly sound. Twinkly lights. The* DANCE FAIRY *appears in a pink tutu, with a magic wand.*]

DANCE FAIRY: I can help you dance.

DOLL: You can?

DANCE FAIRY: That's right. I can make it so you never need to be returned.

[*The* DANCE FAIRY *touches* DOLL *with her magic wand. A twinkly sound. Twinkly lights. Instantly, the* DOLL *does a complicated and beautiful routine.*]

DOLL: Wow, thank you so much—but who are you?

DANCE FAIRY: I'm the Dance Fairy!

DOLL: Wow, thank you so much, Dance Fairy!

DANCE FAIRY: And now, watch this!

[*The* DANCE FAIRY *touches the* DOLL *with her wand. The* DOLL *does an amazing ballet routine, including pirouettes, arabesques, deep bows, and so on.*]

DOLL: Wow!

DANCE FAIRY: Do you think you could say "Thank you, Dance Fairy" again?

DOLL: Sure! Thank you, Dance Fairy. I'm so happy. Now I know I won't be returned!

DANCE FAIRY: Do you think you could say it again?

DOLL: I guess. [*Hesitating.*] Um, thank you. [*Pause.*] This is creeping me out.

DANCE FAIRY: Do you think you could possibly say "Thank you, Dance Fairy" every single minute of your day? Like when your person takes you off the shelf or when she puts you back on the shelf or when you are just resting *on* the shelf, or at night when she turns out the light, or in the morning when the sun comes up and the rays touch you—do you think you could possibly say "Thank you, Dance Fairy" every waking moment of your day? And maybe some of the sleeping moments, too?

DOLL: No. I don't want to say "Thank you, Dance Fairy" every minute.

DANCE FAIRY: But I'm the one. The one who taught you this amazing dance. I'm the one who's keeping you from being returned.

DOLL: No, I'm sorry. But I can't. Thank you again for all the amazing steps you showed me. But if I can't do them on my own, what good are they? If I have to be returned, I'll be returned.

DANCE FAIRY: Well, if that's the way you feel about it . . .

[*Lights darken. Thunder sounds. The* DANCE FAIRY *turns and turns until she vanishes in a tornado of a pirouette.*]

DOLL: Good-bye, Dance Fairy. [*The* Box *snores.*] So here I am. All alone. Let's see what I can do. [*She tries the fancy routines the* DANCE FAIRY *gave her, but she can only remember a part of them. She's getting incredibly frustrated. She stops. She waits. She finds her own dance as the sun comes up.*] Wow. Thank you, Sun. [*The* Box *snores.*] And of course, Box. Thank you, Air. And ground. Even that weird, needy Dance Fairy. Thank you all. Muchisimas gracias. Merci. Merci. [*She sings.*]

Merci
Merci
Thank you sky and thank you floor
Everything that came before
Everything that brought this moment
Home to me
Merci, merci

Thank you night
And thank you box
Thank you ringing morning clocks
Sunlight shining light on me
Everything I'm gonna be—
Merci, merci
Merci, merci

It takes a little bit of magic
And a lot of follow-through
To keep feet and fingers dancing
When you don't know what to do—

But now you do!

So thank you stuck
And thank you scared
And thanks for
Coming unprepared—
This mystery
Merci, merci
Merci, merci

BOX: [*Yawning awake.*] Was that you singing?

DOLL: [*Suddenly shy.*] Mmhm.

Box: What's up, buttercup? Got the stuff, powder puff? I can't wait! It's almost time. When they put in my battery and I can go POW CACHUFF CACHING VOLLY-OOP SPLAT CACHIZ BOOM!!POW POW POW POW— WOOO-OOP!

Doll: It turned out I don't need a battery.

[*She dances.*]

Little Girl: [*Voice from offstage.*] Look, Mom, look! She's dancing!

Different Friends

Paige Steadman

Comic

TAYLOR: 7 to 10, a girl
LEE: 7 to 10, a boy
SUMMER: 7 to 10, a girl

TAYLOR *has walked into a new elementary school.* LEE *is the popular kid.* SUMMER *is not very popular.* TAYLOR *has befriended both* LEE *and* SUMMER, *but that doesn't mean that* LEE *and* SUMMER *get along well. They are on the playground.* LEE *is bouncing a ball.* TAYLOR *and* SUMMER *enter.*

TAYLOR: Hi, Lee!

LEE: I didn't say you could bring her.

SUMMER: Fine. I'll go.

TAYLOR: Summer is my friend, too.

LEE: You're my friend.

SUMMER: No, she's my friend.

LEE: She's my friend. You're different.

TAYLOR: We can all be friends. Please. Let's try it!

LEE: [*Walks over to* SUMMER.] You don't smell bad today.

TAYLOR: Lee!

SUMMER: Thanks?

LEE: [*To* TAYLOR.] What? I said something nice. [*He tosses the ball to* TAYLOR, *who tosses it to* SUMMER, *who puts the ball down.*]

SUMMER: I don't want to play ball. I want to play pretend.

TAYLOR: Ooh, okay. We could play house?

LEE: Bo-ring!

SUMMER: Let's play adventure! Like once upon a time, and fairy tales and rescues.

LEE: Okay! I'll be the big, nasty ogre, and Taylor is the princess in the castle, and you can be the knight.

TAYLOR: I guess.

SUMMER: [*To* LEE.] You don't want to be the knight?

LEE: I'll be the big, nasty ogre.

SUMMER: Ogres are scary!

TAYLOR: He could be a dragon instead.

LEE: A dragon. This is my lair.

TAYLOR: And this is my castle! Ooh, that's tall. Summer, will you give me a hand up there?

SUMMER: I don't want to play this way.

TAYLOR: Then what do you want?

LEE: Rarrrr! I'm the big, nasty dragon, come to kill everyone in the castle!

TAYLOR: Oh brave knight, defend me!

SUMMER: Defend yourself. [*She goes off to the side and sits, pouting.*]

LEE: Rarr! Hiss! My flames will burn the castle!

TAYLOR: Dragon, wait!

LEE: Huh?

TAYLOR: Dragon, why do you want to hurt princesses?

LEE: It's tradition! That's what all dragons do!

TAYLOR: Well that's species-ist.

LEE: Huh?

TAYLOR: Come, thou awful, fiery beast, and, and, and listen to a maiden's mourningful plea.

LEE: What?

TAYLOR: That's tradition, too.

LEE: Oh. Okay.

TAYLOR: Dragon, I'm awf'lly worried about my lady knight.

LEE: Why should the dragon care?

TAYLOR: It's another maiden in danger. Besides. The princess will start crying!

LEE: Oh no, don't do that.

TAYLOR: Dragon, help me find my knight.

LEE: She's just being different.

TAYLOR: You say that like it's bad. I don't get you sometimes. We're different from each other.

LEE: That's . . . it's . . . oh fine. Come on. [LEE *helps* TAYLOR *step down from her perch.* LEE *and* TAYLOR *go over to* SUMMER.]

LEE: Summer? Why didn't you join us?

SUMMER: It doesn't matter.

TAYLOR: Yeah, it does.

LEE: Are you mad at us?

SUMMER: I never get to be the princess!

TAYLOR: You wanted to be the princess?

LEE: Why didn't you just say so?

TAYLOR: We can do that! I wanted to be the knight, anyway.

LEE: Why didn't you say so?

TAYLOR: I dunno.

SUMMER: I can be the princess?

TAYLOR: Yeah!

LEE: Okay. You can be the princess.

SUMMER: I want a blue dress. Blue is my favorite color.

TAYLOR: It's your princess dress.

LEE: Dresses? Doesn't matter to me. Look, it's starting to get dark.

SUMMER: I . . . I guess I feel a little silly.

TAYLOR: Me, too.

LEE: We should go home.

[SUMMER *and* TAYLOR *look at him expectantly.*]

LEE: What?

TAYLOR: Never mind.

SUMMER: Hey, guys? Let's try this again tomorrow.

TAYLOR: Yeah. And next time, I get to be the knight!

Drown

David Hilder

Dramatic

ALISON: 12
JEREMY: 12

JEREMY *and* ALISON *are going to a Halloween party. Their friendship has been tested, though, by the fact that* JEREMY'*s mother committed suicide less than 3 months earlier.* ALISON *is not sure how to talk to* JEREMY *anymore, and* JEREMY *is of course dealing with his own grief as best he can; his homework has suffered, and* ALISON *does not approve. In a way, she serves as his conscience while he grapples with the enormity and complexity of what has happened. Outside* ALISON'*s house.* JEREMY *is dressed as a devil, in a pretty fantastic homemade costume—a red hoodie, with red horns attached to the hood, which is currently down, and flames painted on his jeans. He has fat black lines drawn on his face with makeup—maybe they radiate out from his eyes—and they make him look sad and scary. He paces.* ALISON *comes out as a weird princess. She looks pretty great, but she's not transformed like* JEREMY *is.*

ALISON: Wow!

JEREMY: You, too.

ALISON: Put your hood up. [*He obliges.*] That is a really cool costume.

JEREMY: Thanks. Yours, too.

ALISON: This is dumb. I mean, I look pretty good? But the costume's kind of obvious. Yours is awesome.

JEREMY: Had to do something while I wasn't writing that paper.

ALISON: What'd your dad say about that? Did he—You want to walk? [JEREMY *nods; she yells back into her house.*] MOM, JEREMY AND I ARE LEAVING, I'LL BE HOME BY 11:30. WE'RE AT CONSTANCE YARROW'S HOUSE ON OAKDALE. [*She returns.*] Okay. So what'd he say?

JEREMY: He hasn't said anything.

ALISON: You didn't tell him? [JEREMY *shakes his head no.*] I thought you had to write it before you could come tonight. [JEREMY *is silent.*] Oh, my GOD—you told him you wrote it when you didn't?!

JEREMY: Yes.

ALISON: Jeremy! That is . . . [*She shakes her head as they walk.*] Didn't Mrs. Reardon call him or anything?

JEREMY: I don't know. I don't think they call your parents if you get a bad grade in middle school.

ALISON: You didn't get a bad grade, Jeremy. You got a zero.

JEREMY: Right, thanks, I forgot . . .

ALISON: Wow. [*A breath.*] Let's just have fun at a party. They have a huge house.

JEREMY: Yeah, I know.

ALISON: What, have you been there?

JEREMY: No, I just know where she lives . . . take a pill.

ALISON: You take a pill.

JEREMY: No, thank you.

ALISON: Fine. No pills for us. Ha-rumph.

JEREMY: You're crazy.

ALISON: Yep! Batshit Bonkers from Crazytown, that's me! The little lady who used to set the ends of her own hair on fire before yanking it out!

JEREMY: Those were good times.

ALISON: They were. We were so innocent then. [*They just walk for a bit.*] I like the fire paint you did on your jeans. You must've spent a lot of allowance on paint.

JEREMY: Actually, we had this stuff left over from last year, so . . .

ALISON: Fire pants. And red horns. [*She laughs to herself.*] I told you my jeans story, right? From last year? [JEREMY *shakes his head no.*] OH!!! Oh, my God, so, okay, so my mom, last year, we were shopping for clothes, and I'm trying on jeans. And this one pair of jeans looked really good. And I come out of the dressing room, and my mom and I are in total agreement, and they're not too expensive, and we're all set to buy these jeans when I get my period. Like, my first period. Ever. Of my life.

Jeremy: Got it.

Alison: And it's horrible, but, ya know, at least we were going to buy the jeans! And it's gross, and I'm crying, like, really snotty crying, because—this will never happen to you, but just so you know? Getting your period in the dressing room at Kohl's is about the most humiliating thing that can happen to a person.

Jeremy: Okay.

Alison: And my mom, my MOM, starts CLAPPING AND LAUGHING, Jeremy!

Jeremy: No way.

Alison: She does! And then she starts asking around for a maxi pad, just, you know, ASKING TOTAL STRANGERS. She asks literally every woman within earshot for a MAXI PAD for her LITTLE GIRL WHO IS RIGHT NOW GETTING HER FIRST PERIOD IN DRESSING ROOM SIX!

Jeremy: Oh, my God.

Alison: At Kohl's!! I don't think I've ever cried that much in my life. And she didn't understand why I was furious, which just—Oh! And then when she was telling my father about it, I was up in my room, so angry, and from my room I actually heard her say, "She's going through a phase, that's all." A PHASE?! You broadcast my menstruation to the entire population of a discount department store, you BITCH! [*They both laaaaaaaaugh!*]

JEREMY: Oh, my God. That SUCKS. It's totally gross but it sucks.

ALISON: Like, there has never been a suckier moment in my life so far than that one.

JEREMY: Yeah. [*They walk, laugh, settle into not laughing anymore.*]

ALISON: I guess it's . . . I mean, it's not on the same level or anything, as what your . . .

JEREMY: [*Stopping short.*] Don't.

ALISON: I'm sorry.

JEREMY: Don't try to . . . relate, or whatever! Okay? God!

ALISON: I thought we were, ya know . . . on the same page for half a second!

JEREMY: We were until you tried to get all inside my head about it!

ALISON: Okay! [*She starts to walk, stops, turns back to him.*] I don't like this, you know. I don't like that you get to decide when we get to be funny and when we have to be serious and what we can and can't talk about. It's really crappy for me.

JEREMY: It's really crappy for YOU?!

ALISON: It's really crappy for me, TOO! Is what I meant! Your thing affects people!

JEREMY: I'm sorry!

ALISON: Don't say you're sorry! Just . . . God, just let me know when I'm allowed to breathe around you again. I look forward to the day, is all. Jeez. [*They stand there, not looking at each other, a princess and a devil.*]

JEREMY: You still want to go?

ALISON: No. But I'm gonna. Because I have to see people see you in that costume.

JEREMY: Okay. Thanks.

ALISON: [*Still mad.*] You're welcome.

JEREMY: That's nice of you.

ALISON: [*Still mad.*] You're welcome. Come on.

Eleven and Eight

Ellen Koivisto

Dramatic

ELEVEN: a female
EIGHT: a male

Anytime, anyplace.

ELEVEN: Get down.

EIGHT: No.

ELEVEN: Get down.

EIGHT: No. [ELEVEN *pulls him down.*] No! [EIGHT *jumps back up.*] No!

ELEVEN: Shut up! [*Pulls* EIGHT *down again.*] Shut up! [*Puts her hand over his mouth.*]

EIGHT: [*Muffled.*] Stop it! Stop it! [*Kicking.*]

[ELEVEN *sits on* EIGHT.]

ELEVEN: [*Punching for punctuation.*] Shut up. Shut up. Shut up. Shut up. Shut up. You better shut up. You better right now. Shut up. Right now. Stop it. Stop it. Just stop it. Be quiet and I'll take my hand off. I will. [*Panting.*] I'll take my hand off if you stay down and stay quiet. Stay quiet. Or they'll hear you and kill you. And I'll let them. Will you be quiet? Will you?

[EIGHT *nods.* ELEVEN *takes hand off slowly, then slowly gets off* EIGHT. EIGHT *kicks her hard while rolling to get up.* ELEVEN *moans.*]

EIGHT: Don't make any noise. They'll hear you. [*Pause.*] You're not hurt. [*Pause.*] I'm hurt. [*Pause.*] I think you broke something punching me.

ELEVEN: I broke my knuckles.

EIGHT: No. I mean it. It hurts here, bad.

ELEVEN: I didn't break anything. I didn't, but they will when they get you. They'll break you up into little pieces. They'll put a knife through you, right there.

EIGHT: No, they won't.

ELEVEN: You make too much noise.

EIGHT: They do worse to girls.

ELEVEN: You know what they do to noisy boys? They cut off their ears, snik, snik, and then their noses, glush, and then their arms, one at a time, chuk, chuk, and then their legs, and then their—

EIGHT: I saw what they do to girls. I saw it.

ELEVEN: If the girls are noisy, it's just the same.

EIGHT: No, it isn't. It's worse. I know. I saw it.

ELEVEN: No, you didn't. You didn't see anything.

EIGHT: Yes, I did. I saw them . . . I saw it.

ELEVEN: No, you didn't. Liar.

EIGHT: I did.

ELEVEN: No! No, no, no. Liar. Liar!

EIGHT: You shut up. [*Punches* ELEVEN.] Shut up.

ELEVEN: Don't you lie like that again.

EIGHT: I'm not lying. I saw them with my sisters, I saw them.

ELEVEN: If you don't be quiet, I'll leave you.

EIGHT: I saw it.

ELEVEN: I'll go. I really will.

EIGHT: My sisters screamed.

ELEVEN: I won't stay if you talk. I'll go. I'm going.

EIGHT: My stomach hurts. Where you punched me. You broke something.

ELEVEN: They just kill, that's all, they kill everyone, girls and boys, the same.

EIGHT: It hurts. Owww.

ELEVEN: They do. Shh . . .

EIGHT: It hurts.

ELEVEN: Shhhh!

EIGHT: What?

ELEVEN: Do you hear that?

EIGHT: Yes. Oh.

ELEVEN: Oh, God. Oh, God. Shut up!

[*She dives to cover him, and they huddle as small as they can.*]

Enter Bogart

The Most Spectacularly Misfit Adventure in the History of High School Crime

Jacqueline Goldfinger and
Jennifer MacMillan

Comic

FALCON: 13
SAM: 13
JANELLE: 13

All the characters are girls.

*SAM and FALCON are on a mission to find a third student to add
to their crime-investigating team. FALCON picks up a magic
eight ball from a box next to her. She shakes it and concentrates.
They meet JANELLE.*

FALCON: Will we ever find a third person who will help us
solve this mystery? [*Flips it over and reads.*] It is decidedly
so!

[*There is a knock at the door. It is JANELLE POPADOPALINSKI—
aka Head Gear Girl who has a lisp due to her orthodontics. She
opens the door gingerly—pokes her head in.*]

JANELLE: Am I too late? I got thuck in Civics. Like actually rather literally thuck. Ith a long thory. I won't bother you. Here. [*She hands* FALCON *her resume, who examines it quickly and excitedly passes it off to* SAM. SAM *examines it. Sniffs it.*]

SAM: Smells like . . . coffee. And . . . doughnuts?

JANELLE: Oh right! Here, I brought you the, the . . . [*Pulls coffee and doughnuts from her backpack.*] I don't know. I jutht figured you guyth were in here all afternoon and well . . . I heard the choir's audition becauthe I mean, how could you not, am I right? And I just thought . . . Be a team member! Be a team member, Janelle Popadopalinthki, and go the extra mile!

FALCON: Wow! Boston crème. The good stuff! [*She goes to take a bite and* SAM *slaps it out of her hand.*]

SAM: Um. Well thank you for those, but let's talk about your qualifications.

JANELLE: Oh yeth, of course. Well, I livh with my grandmother. She's raithing me. And well she lotht her glaththeth and her inhaler and her dentureth all the time. I always find them. Even when they're in the freezer or in the glove box of the old '79 Thingray that's on blocks in our front yard. It doethn't run but . . .

FALCON: A '79 Stingray?!? You have a '79 . . .

SAM: Well. I'm not sure that's really enough, um, qualifications, see? I mean it takes a lot to be a detective. Cunning, stealth, superior intelligence—

JANELLE: Here. [JANELLE *picks up the giant ring of school keys that the janitor left behind.*]

SAM: What's that? Some old keys to . . . [*It dawns of her.*] Holy cow, Batman. These keys, these keys open . . .

[*The three share a look.*]

SAM, FALCON, and JANELLE: Everything!

JANELLE: And then I said to myself, "Janelle Popadopalinthki, make a list of poththible thuspectth! That will wow them!" But then I said, "No Popadopalinthki, make the litht, but then whittle it down! Do the rethearch! Go for the Gold! Be the change you withh to thee in the world!"

[*She hands over a short list to* SAM.]

SAM: Wow. This is. A pretty decent start. And Bridget and Thursby are at the top of our list, too. But what about your ability to be stealthy. I mean . . . your . . . your um . . . [*She points to the headgear.*] . . . I'm sorry. It's just . . .

JANELLE: No. No it'th okay. My headgear. You can thay it. It'th not tho bad actually. Other than having to thleep on it at night. But it'th thort of helpful becauthe no one theeth me. No one really ever lookth at me. I think they think they'll embarrathth me if they look at me and it. At firtht it wath kind of hard but then I noticed. I could go placeth, blend in, be everyone and no one. Be everywhere and nowhere.

SAM: Thanks for coming in.

JANELLE: [*Crestfallen as they push her out the door.*] Oh. That'th it? I mean I can . . . I can . . . anthwer some more interview quethtionth. I have a 3.957 GPA. I can drive a car. I'm a polymathhhhhhh!

SAM: That's great. Thanks so much. We'll just [*She's ushering* JANELLE *out.*] call you—if we need you—at some point in time. But don' call us, you see, we're pretty busy, and um, hard to find really, hard to pin down, all that slinking about the shadows and stuff, and so, happy holidays and um, drive safe.

JANELLE: [*From the doorway.*] Um, but, okay, bye!

[*A beat.* SAM *sighs. Exhausted. And then from offstage we hear:*]

JANELLE: Very few of uth are what we seem. That'th Agatha Chrithie.

[SAM *looks to* FALCON.]

FALCON: I don't do an English accent.

SAM: Phew. That was close.

FALCON: [*Double-fisting doughnuts.*] I don't know. She was funny. She has some real guts. I think she was the best candidate for the job.

SAM: That's only because we had no quality candidates. What's going on here?

FALCON: Yeah, good question. What is going on here, Sam?

SAM: All right, well . . . truth?

Falcon: Truth.

Sam: She's . . . she's a weirdo. She's embarrassing. I mean, sure she's nice and everything. And smart. And helpful.

Falcon: [*With a mouth full.*] And doughnuts!

Sam: But once we hire her, we have to sit with her at lunch [*Or insert the name of your free period here*]. And it's a slippery slope from there, my friend. We'll end up on her dodgeball team [*Or insert other sport name here.*] in gym! And after that no one will ask us to the Winter Formal, not if they think Head Gear Girl is going to tag along. And who can blame them really?

Falcon: I guess you're right. We can't really hire her. It's not our fault. Our hands are tied here. She'll understand that, I'm sure. Right? Right? I mean, she did notice the janitor's keys that will get us into Mr. A's room. And she did have a list of suspects. And she did bring the snacks but . . .

Sam: [*Unsure.*] We'll be fine alone.

Falcon: We have ideas.

Sam: We have observations. Just the two of us.

[*A beat.*]

Falcon: Just the two of us. Like Han Solo and Chewbacca!

[*A quick beat.*]

Sam and Falcon: I'm Han!

SAM and **FALCON:** No. I'm HAN.

SAM and **FALCON:** I'm. NO. I'm.

SAM: Never mind. Just the two of us.

FALCON: Yeah! Like Sherlock and Watson!

SAM and **FALCON:** I'M

SAM and **FALCON:** Uggghhhh! I'M. NO. YOUR. I'M SHERLOCK! [*A beat.*] Let's just investigate.

Escape
from *Once Upon a Teenager*

Claudia I. Haas

Comic

DOROTHY: 7 to 8
EDGAR: 10, DOROTHY's older brother

DOROTHY is determined to run away from home. She has a satchel that has 2 sticks, a bedsheet, a jar with cookies, a small soup pot and spoon, a penny, a teabag, a dress, and a doll.

DOROTHY: Fare-thee-well, farmhouse! I am never stepping inside you again! They'll be sorry when I'm gone! I wish I could stay so I could hear how sorry they all are!

[EDGAR *enters.*]

EDGAR: Dorothy!

DOROTHY: Drat! Edgar's such a pest! Better scram!

EDGAR: I see you!

DOROTHY: If you come near me, I'll kick and I'll bite and you can't make me stay!

EDGAR: Oh, I'm not going to make you stay.

DOROTHY: You're not?

EDGAR: No. I just want to make sure you have everything you need for your journey.

DOROTHY: I do!

EDGAR: Can I see? So I can reassure Mom and Dad?

DOROTHY: I . . . guess.

EDGAR: [*Takes out a doll.*] Now, you need food and shelter but definitely not a doll!

DOROTHY: Esmeralda takes care of me! Especially when all of you pester me! And I have food, see? [*She takes out a small jar of cookies.*] And I have a tent.

EDGAR: That looks like a sheet.

DOROTHY: Well, Mr. Know-it-all, I have two sticks. I'll just stick them in the ground and put the sheet over it and I will have my own sheet-home. See, I thought of everything.

EDGAR: [*Taking out a penny.*] Oh! And you brought money. Good thinking!

DOROTHY: I'm not going to spend that! That's my lucky penny. I rubbed it every day that Dad was gone. And he came home safe. It's good luck.

EDGAR: Oh! You can't take Mom's soup pot! And her spoon!

DOROTHY: It's old and I need it to cook stuff.

EDGAR: What can you cook?

DOROTHY: Well, smarty-pants, I can cook dandelion soup. So there!

EDGAR: Who's going to pick the ants out of the dandelions?

DOROTHY: What?

EDGAR: Ants love dandelions. They get inside the buds and refuse to come out. You don't like ants.

DOROTHY: I know! I'll have to make grass soup then. Rain water and grass—delicious!

EDGAR: And when the snow comes and covers the grass?

DOROTHY: [*Taking out a tea bag.*] I'll melt the snow and make tea! Ice tea.

EDGAR: Well, you sure did think of everything. What do you want me tell Mom in case she cries or something?

DOROTHY: She won't cry. She hardly knows I'm around. She's so busy working.

EDGAR: And Dad?

DOROTHY: Dad's busy with college. He doesn't notice me anymore.

EDGAR: Dorothy! He has to go—it's free for all the soldiers.

DOROTHY: I know that. I hear that a thousand times every day! With Mom gone all day and Dad gone day at night, I'm stuck inside doing all the chores. You get to be in the fields and I'm never outside! The world is passing me by while I sit inside and sweep the floors. You treat me like Cinderella!

EDGAR: So . . . you're thinking if you run away—you'll find your prince?

DOROTHY: Don't need no stinking prince.

EDGAR: What about Socks? He's going to be so lonely without you. With Mom working, Dad at school, and all us boys in the fields, who's going to take of Socks? That was your job.

DOROTHY: I know.

EDGAR: So, you're just going to abandon your beloved kitty-cat. That's an awful thing to do!

DOROTHY: You'll take care of him, won't you?

EDGAR: I'll try. But after school and chores, well, I may just forget. But that's fine—run away. Leave Socks to meow at your door every night waiting for you to come home. Leave him to die of a broken heart. It's your choice. [*He exits.*]

DOROTHY: *Edgar!* [*She picks up her stuff.*] I was this close to making my escape. Now I'm stuck in the house being Cinderella to an ungrateful family! Socks? Ohhhh, Socks! [*She exits.*]

Frankenfish

Steven Schutzman

Seriocomic

JOE: 14, a charming upstate New York farm boy.
HANNA: 14, a girl from New York City.

Note: The first syllable of HANNA is pronounced with a schwa a: Hah-na, as in "fä-ther."

Twilight. At a pond in upstate New York, HANNA, *in a swimsuit, has just been swimming and is drying herself and putting her clothes back on, with* JOE *watching her from some distance away. Unseen,* JOE *saunters up from behind.*

JOE: Hello.

HANNA: [*Startled.*] Huh!

JOE: I said, hello.

HANNA: God, you scared me.

JOE: Didn't mean to.

HANNA: You shouldn't sneak up on people like that.

JOE: Sorry. Guess you're all nervous like.

HANNA: You snuck up on me.

JOE: Jumpy. [*He grins at her.*]

HANNA: [*Deciding he's harmless, playfully.*] Go away.

JOE: I see you been swimmin'.

HANNA: Oh, really? You figured that out?

JOE: Hair all wet.

HANNA: No, a rainstorm rained on me, from my own personal rain cloud.

JOE: 'Fact, I was watchin' you swim.

HANNA: Oh, a peeping Tom.

JOE: Name's Joe. And yours is?

HANNA: Hanna.

JOE: [*Playing with her, pronouncing her name correctly, with a schwa a, as in "father."*] Hanna? Hanna? [*Then,*] Oh, you mean Hah-na. [*Here, he pronounces the first syllable of her name with a short a, as in "Suzanna," "Louisiana," or "Montana."*]

HANNA: No, Hanna. [*She pronounces her name with a schwa a, as in "father."*]

JOE: Never heard of it.

HANNA: I'm sure there are a lot of things you never . . .

JOE: [*Interrupting playfully.*] Heard of "Han-na" like in "Suzanna" or "Louisiana" or "Montana." Hannah Montana.

HANNA: She is so yesterday, Joe.

JOE: Banana.

HANNA: It's "Hanna," like in "piranha." [*She bares her teeth at him. He laughs.*]

JOE: Joe like in Joe. Hanna. [*He sticks his hand out to shake and she tentatively takes his hand and they shake.*] Pleased to meet you.

HANNA: Hi.

JOE: [*Beat. Beat. He lets go of her hand. Beat. Beat. Then as he watches her struggle to put her skinny jeans on.*] Hard to get a wet foot through a skinny leg hole, Haaa-na.

HANNA: [*Hopping around on one foot to get her skinny jeans on.*] I can do it.

JOE: [*Grinning.*] Need some help?

HANNA: Right. [*She sits down in order to get it done.*]

JOE: Stupid pants, you can't get 'em on without a fight.

HANNA: You're right. [*She does it.*] There. [*Beat. Beat. It seems to get darker.*] What was that?

JOE: Sun just dropped behind the hills. Shadows takin' over. Soon there'll be a chill in the air. Chill comes on fast when you lose the sun.

HANNA: Oh.

JOE: And you all wet. [*They sit in a comfortable silence. Beat. Beat.*] You're pretty brave for a city girl, Hanna. Swimmin' here by yourself.

HANNA: How do you know I'm from the city?

JOE: How does a person know a bear is from the woods?

HANNA: Is it that obvious?

JOE: New York City, right?

HANNA: Right.

JOE: I knew that. The accent, the sarcasm, the personal rain cloud, the suspicious look, Hanna, the skinny jeans, all jumpy. You got New York City pourin' out your pores and beamin' out your eyeballs. I can hear subway trains roarin' through the canyons of your head, and such.

HANNA: [*She likes him.*] Oh, yeah. [*Beat.*] I'm visiting my uncle.

JOE: I knew that. [*Pause.*] There's another reason I knew right away you weren't from 'round here. 'Cause people 'round here don't swim in this pond 'counta the Frankenfish.

HANNA: Okay.

JOE: Frankenfish. [*He begins a Frankenfish imitation, stumbling around like Frankenstein's monster for a few seconds.*]

HANNA: Okay, I'll bite. What's a Frankenfish?

JOE: Frankenfish like Frankenstein's monster, stumblin' around the village, all different parts sewn together, brain from a jar. [*Really stumbling around like Frankenstein's monster.*] Aaaaggghhh!

HANNA: You are funny.

JOE: Frankenfish. Razor-sharp teeth. Latches on, doesn't let go. Walks on land. Came here all the way from China.

HANNA: Walked here from China? I don't think so.

JOE: They got imported as pets, let loose by the pet owners, and infested the local waters, includin' this pond.

HANNA: Okay.

JOE: And at night . . . like it's gonna be soon, Hanna . . . them fish walk the roads goin' from pond to pond and creek to creek in the dark—sometimes herds of 'em, ferocious herds of 'em—in the dark.

HANNA: I better watch my step.

JOE: Better. [*Watching her struggle to put a sock on.*] Hard to get a sock on a wet foot.

HANNA: [*Imitating his accent.*] You're just full of pearls of wisdom, ain't ya?

JOE: I guess. Frankenfish bite something terrible in the water. I was just hangin' 'round here 'case I had to save you from drownin' or bleedin' to death.

HANNA: Thank you, Joe.

JOE: Just in case. People in the country, farm people, watch out for each other. Do unto others. Not like in New York City. And now, with the sun goin' down, and herds 'a them Frankenfish roamin' the roads, you're gonna need an escort home, to your uncle's.

HANNA: Really.

JOE: I'd say.

HANNA: Okay. Okay. Just let me tie my shoes. [*She does.*] There. [*She stands.*] I'm ready now. Think we'll make it, Joe?

JOE: Maybe. Might. But stick close to me. I hear they can really jump. [*They hold hands and start to walk off together.*]

Gathering Blue

Eric Coble

Dramatic

THOMAS: 15
KIRA: 15

In a dystopian future, KIRA, *a recent orphan, has just been pulled from the savage wilderness by the Guardians to become the official Weaver of her community. In her new luxurious room, she meets* THOMAS, *the official Carver for the Guardians.*

THOMAS: Kira?

KIRA: . . . yes?

THOMAS: Kira the Threader. They told me you had come.

KIRA: You're the Carver?

THOMAS: Thomas. [*Beat.*] My workroom is across the hall. And my room. I live and work in the room across the hall.

KIRA: This is my live and workroom.

[*Beat.*]

THOMAS: Your worktable is under a window—that's good.

KIRA: The light is good, yes.

THOMAS: And have you used your tub?

KIRA: What?

THOMAS: The

KIRA: No. It just seems such a bother when the stream's so nearby.

THOMAS: The tenders will show you how it works.

KIRA: Tenders?

THOMAS: The ones who bring you food. They'll help you however you want. And then a Guardian will be checking on you every day.

KIRA: Every day?

THOMAS: They need to make sure the work is progressing.

[*Pause.*]

KIRA: So how long have you lived here?

THOMAS: Since I was quite young. Ever since I could make pictures with a sharp tool and a piece of wood. Everyone thought it was "amazing."

KIRA: And your parents let you come live with the Guardians?

THOMAS: They don't care.

KIRA: Really?

THOMAS: They're not here. They were killed in a storm.

KIRA: Oh no.

THOMAS: [*Shrugs.*] Lightning.

KIRA: How? People don't go out in thunderstorms.

THOMAS: They were on some sort of errand.

KIRA: Were you there? How did you stay safe?

THOMAS: I was alone at the hut. Some Guardians came and got me and told me. I'm just lucky they thought my work was of value, or I would have been given away. I've been here ever since. [KIRA *nods.*] So far I've just been practicing, making ornaments for many of the Guardians. Now, though, I do real work. Important work.

KIRA: Doing what?

THOMAS: Carving the Singer's Staff. For the Ruin Song. They've given me wonderful tools.

[*A bell rings somewhere.*]

KIRA: That usually means it's time to go to work.

THOMAS: [*Shrugs.*] It doesn't matter. There are no real rules here. As long as the work gets done by the Gathering.

Gathering Blue

Eric Coble

Dramatic

MATT: 10
KIRA: 15

In a dystopian future, KIRA, *an orphan, has just been pulled from the savage wilderness by the Guardians to become the official Weaver of her community. She now ventures back out into the dangerous forest to meet her new mentor, accompanied by her rough-and-tumble friend from childhood,* MATT.

MATT: Is be coming too.

KIRA: Matt—

MATT: You be needing a protector. Them woods is full of fierce creatures.

KIRA: Protector? You?

MATT: I only look wee.

KIRA: Jamison said it was safe as long as I stay on the path.

MATT: But suppose you get lost. I can find my way out of anywheres.

KIRA: I'll be gone all day. You'll get hungry.

MATT: [*Pulls a wad of bread from his pants pocket.*] I filched this crusty from the baker.

[*Beat. KIRA looks at MATT.*]

KIRA: Fine. You and your wad of bread can be my protectors.

MATT: Yes! [*Lights shift and they start out.*] Probably be snakes all in here.

KIRA: I'm not afraid of snakes.

MATT: Most girls be.

KIRA: Not me. There were always small snakes in my mother's garden. She said they were friends to the plants. They ate bugs.

MATT: Like that bug there. That be called a daddy longlegs.

KIRA: [*Laughs.*] I wonder whose daddy it is?

MATT: Not mine.

KIRA: Do you have a father?

MATT: Did. Now my ma is all I got.

KIRA: What happened to your father?

MATT: [*Shrugs.*] Dunno. In the part of the village where you growed, things is different, but in the Fen where I live, most gots no pa. And them that got 'em wish they didn't, 'cause they hit something horrid. But my ma hits, too. Hard. I told her if she ever did it again I was leaving for evers.

KIRA: Where would you go?

MATT: Dunno. The Wild. Far away. Somewheres no one would ever find me again.

KIRA: You mustn't leave your mother. You should be thankful every day you have a parent.

MATT: Hard to remember when blood be coming out my cheek where she hit.

KIRA: [*Pulls her pendant out.*] You see this?

MATT: It be all purpley. And shiny-like. [*Grabs it.*] Gimme.

KIRA: [*Pulls back.*] Don't! Matt! Don't grab. If you want something, you should ask.

MATT: Gimme is an ask.

KIRA: No it isn't. You should learn some manners.

[MATT *backs off, hurt.*]

KIRA: This was a gift. My father made it as a gift for my mother. And she gave it as a gift to me.

MATT: "Gift"?

KIRA: When you care about someone and give them something special. Something they treasure. That's a "gift."

MATT: So if I give you a gift, you'll like me best of all?

KIRA: I already like you.

MATT: [*Laughs.*] In the Fen they don't got that. Gifts. In the Fen iffen they give you something special, it be a kick in your buttie.

Get to the Point

Fran Handman

Comic

MARTA: 10 to 15
JOSÉ: 10 to 15
CARMEN: 10 to 15
AYISHA: 10 to 15

Note: Characters could alternatively be MARTA, JOSÉ, PEDRO, and CARMEN.

Four kids are hanging around on a stoop.

MARTA: You know, nobody knows how they built the pyramids. But I've got it all figured out.

ALL: Not again!

MARTA: All right, if you don't want to learn anything, that's your tough luck, but I know how it happened.

JOSÉ: Okay, Marta, let's hear it. You're going to tell us anyway.

MARTA: There was this woman who was a stargazer. She'd watch the stars and check for eclipses, and so on.

CARMEN: What does that have to do with the pyramids?

MARTA: Hold your horses. I'm getting to it. Well, this woman watched the sky from land and from sea, any way she could. She'd even get into her rowboat so she could watch the stars in different positions.

AYISHA: Ah, come on, Marta. Where was she rowing her boat? The pyramids are in the desert. What was she doing, rowing her boat on the sand?

MARTA: Were you there? That was a long time ago. How do you know there wasn't a lake?

AYISHA: You're right. How would I know that?

MARTA: Anyway, one night she notices a big square rock in the water. She had never seen it before, and she knew that section of the water backward and forward.

JOSÉ: A rock, huh?

MARTA: She also noticed that there was a full moon. . . .

CARMEN: That explains it—full moon—crazy people.

MARTA: You gonna listen or not? Anyway, there's this full moon and she figured that the moon had something to do with the rock. She was really dumbfounded.

CARMEN: Dumbfounded—ooh, I like that word. Dumbfounded.

MARTA: You know, Carmen, you are one looney bird.

JOSÉ: So what does the moon have to do with a rock?

MARTA: The pull of gravity. You've heard that the moon affects the tides. That's the way things are today. In those days the moon was stronger.

AYISHA: Where did you hear that?

MARTA: It's logical. The moon had to be stronger, because it pulled this big rock right out of the water.

CARMEN: That's only one rock, Marta. One rock does not a pyramid make.

MARTA: You don't know anything, Carmen. Let me tell you how the moon works. It keeps shifting position. The next month, when the moon was full again, it pulled out a different rock in a different place. Before you know it, there was a bunch of square rocks all standing like a platform in the water.

JOSÉ: That still isn't a pyramid, Marta.

MARTA: What a bunch of ignoramuses you are. I'm not finished. It gets pretty hot in Egypt, so when that hot sun came out it dried those rocks and they started breaking up into squares.

AYISIIA: But, Marta . . .

MARTA: Then the full moon would come out and pull up the pieces as they broke up until the lightest ones were on top.

JOSÉ: So why aren't the pyramids square? You got an answer for that?

MARTA: Because the moon started losing its strength and wasn't able to pull rocks up easily anymore so it could get fewer and fewer stones up at a time until, finally, the rocks came to a point.

AYISHA: But that's only one pyramid. Where did the others come from?

MARTA: You think I know everything? Maybe the Egyptians thought the first one was so cool, they made two more?

The Great Kitten Caper

Mark Lambeck

Comic

KITTY: 12, the leader
KARLY: 10, the middle sister
PRUDENCE: 8, the practical kitten

When the Three Little Kittens lose their mittens, they decide to frame the Bacon brothers for stealing them, as those Three Little Pigs have a reputation for being bullies. KITTY, KARLY, *and* PRUDENCE *are in a huddle, whispering on center stage.*

KITTY: So, do you guys have the story straight, or do I have to review it again?

KARLY: I'm good. It's brilliant!

[*They both look at* PRUDENCE, *waiting for her response.*]

KITTY: Prudence?

PRUDENCE: I'm thinking.

KITTY: It's not that complicated. But I don't mind going over it again if you're confused.

PRUDENCE: I'm not confused, Kitty. I'm just worried.

KARLY: Here we go. I knew it! I *knew* she would pull something like this.

KITTY: What's the problem?

KARLY: She's a goody two-paws, that's the problem. Mama's little ball of fur. She always has to be the "purr-fect" one.

PRUDENCE: I just don't like lying.

KARLY: Aw. Ya gonna cry now? I hate crying. It's so manipulative.

KITTY: We're not lying. We're just being a little playful with the story. Mama's always sending us out to play. So actually, we're doing exactly what she told us to do, right?

KARLY: Right.

PRUDENCE: But I'm afraid. What if we get caught? Mama will call us "naughty" and we won't get any pie.

KARLY: Oh . . . stop being such a scaredy-cat!

KITTY: We're not gonna get caught. As long as we get the story straight.

KARLY: This is so easy . . . all we have to do is say that the three little Bacon brothers bullied us into giving them our mittens.

KITTY: We all know Mama already doesn't like them. Remember that time she invited them over for lunch?

KARLY: Yeah—they ate like pigs. No table manners at all!

KITTY: And Mama said, "We're never having those Bacon brothers over again, if they can't be civil."

KARLY: She hates bullies and slobs. And she wasn't thrilled about cleaning up the mess they made of her salmon pie. Crumbs and crusts and filling everywhere.

KITTY: And they used their sleeves to wipe their mouths instead of the napkins Mama gave them.

KARLY: Such pigs!

PRUDENCE: But Aunt Fluffy made those mittens for us. Mama said she knitted them special, with tender loving care.

KARLY: Yeah, yeah. We all know Aunt Fluffy is a master with a ball of yarn. But that just proves the point. If Mama finds out we lost those mittens through carelessness, well, there not only won't be any pie, there also won't be any dinner at all.

PRUDENCE: Carelessness? It wasn't carelessness. It was curiosity, Karly. *Your* curiosity.

KARLY: Me? I just wanted to see what was in the bottom of that well. You guys wanted to know, too.

KITTY: That's true, Prudence. We were all curious.

KARLY: But I was the only one courageous enough to lean in for a better look. [*Pause.*] I didn't drop my mittens into it on purpose. They just slipped off. And I wasn't the one who had the brilliant idea of having the two of you throw yours in afterward so we'd all be blamed.

PRUDENCE: I was just trying to cover for you. We're sisters. We need to stick together.

KARLY: Exactly! And that's why we came up with this Bacon brothers story that *you* need to buy into!

PRUDENCE: I thought you'd be grateful if we told Mama that we *all* lost our mittens so she wouldn't just be mad at you! I was trying to protect you.

KARLY: Protect me? The little whiney crybaby was trying to protect me? [*She bursts out laughing and starts coughing. KITTY pats KARLY on the back.*] Man! These hairballs are killing me.

KITTY: Stop it! Both of you! There will be no catfighting—not on my watch.

KARLY: She started it.

PRUDENCE: I'm just telling the truth.

KARLY: Oh. So we're supposed to feel guilty for pointing a paw at those . . . those . . . pigs? Where's your sense of adventure?

PRUDENCE: Where's your conscience?

KARLY: [*Sarcastically.*] "Why don't we all drop our mittens into the well?" Prudence says. And I can't believe you, Kitty. That you went along with such a stupid suggestion.

KITTY: Excuse me! Are you hissing at *me* now? I went along with it because I'm the oldest. I'm the one responsible for you. You two can just go about your day eating, sleeping, and playing carefree, anytime you want. But Mama expects me to watch out for you.

KARLY: I'm not a fraidy cat. I can watch out for myself.

KITTY: No, you can't. I shouldn't have let you walk along the edge of that well. I shouldn't have let you lean over like that. You could have fallen in.

KARLY: But I didn't!

KITTY: And if you had fallen in, it would have been all my fault! You don't know what it's like to have the responsibility.

PRUDENCE: You *do* look out for us, Kitty. And *some* of us really appreciate it.

KARLY: Great. Here she goes again . . .

KITTY: Okay, stop. Now everybody just put away the claws and calm down.

KARLY: Fine. We have a story, so let's just stick to it. Those Bacon brothers deserve whatever they have coming to them.

PRUDENCE: Framing them for a crime they didn't commit? It's dishonest. And that's never pretty.

KITTY: Framing? Do you even know what that means, Prudence?

PRUDENCE: Of course I do. It's blaming someone else for your mistake and then getting others to back you up on it.

KITTY: Wow. That's right! That's pretty good. How did you know . . . ?

PRUDENCE: I may be the youngest, but I can read. Those Nancy Drew mysteries are very educational.

KITTY: Impressive.

KARLY: Then you know that all it takes is a bad reputation. We've all seen the Bacon brothers bully that poor Gingerbread Man. Mama will believe this in a second. I can taste her chicken pot pie now.

KITTY: No. Prudence is right.

KARLY: She is?

PRUDENCE: I am?

KARLY: About what?

KITTY: And you're right too, Karly.

KARLY: Ah-hah! [*Pause.*] But, I'm confused. How can we both be right?

KITTY: It's a good story and Mama would certainly believe the worst of those Bacon bullies. But Prudence is right. It's dishonest. And as the oldest, it's up to me to set the example and take whatever punishment Mama has for me.

KARLY: I don't get it. We have this all worked out. We could pull off this mitten caper in a minute.

KITTY: We probably could, Karly. But we shouldn't. Let's just tell Mama the truth and trust that she'll give us exactly what we deserve.

PRUDENCE: Like homemade pie as a reward for sticking together and telling the truth?

KITTY: It's possible. You never know. [*Holds her paw out in front. She looks to* KARLY *and* PRUDENCE.] Are you in?

PRUDENCE: [*Putting her paw over* KITTY'S.] I'm in. [*They both look at* KARLY, *waiting for a response.*]

KARLY: Ohhh! All for one and one for all, I always say. [*Places her paw on top of the other two.*] I'm in.

ALL THREE TOGETHER: [*They break, lifting their paws and yell.*] Go kittens!

Green Crayon

Rebecca Gorman O'Neill

Comic

CASSIA: 7 to 11
KYLE: 7 to 11

CASSIA sits, drawing on a big piece of paper with crayons. KYLE has a green crayon—the only green crayon.

CASSIA: Green's my favorite color.

KYLE: Mine too.

CASSIA: Give it to me. I need it now.

KYLE: Give what?

CASSIA: I need the green.

KYLE: No.

CASSIA: I can't finish without it.

KYLE: Then you'll never finish.

CASSIA: Give me the green!

KYLE: Never ever ever finish.

CASSIA: You don't need it.

KYLE: Don't matter if I need it.

CASSIA: You're not even drawing.

KYLE: I want it. I have it. I'm keeping it. Don't have to be drawing. Just looking at it, here, in my hand. Makes me all kinds of happy. Don't you want me to be happy?

CASSIA: I'll give it back.

KYLE: You won't.

CASSIA: I will!

KYLE: You won't give it back because you'll never have it in the first place. It's mine.

CASSIA: I'll give you all the others. The reds and the blues and the purples—look at the purples! I'll give you all these if you give me the green.

KYLE: Shouldn't have let it go if you wanted it so much.

CASSIA: I didn't know I wanted it till you had it.

KYLE: Should have planned ahead.

CASSIA: Keep it then. I don't need it. I can just mash the blues in with the yellows. [*She tries this.*]

KYLE: Oooh . . . That's not working so well, is it?

CASSIA: How was I supposed to know, way back then, that I would need it now? Way back then when I started? I couldn't have known I'd want it.

KYLE: But now you do.

CASSIA: Now I really, really do.

KYLE: Maybe this is a lesson.

CASSIA: A lesson.

KYLE: You know what a metaphor is?

CASSIA: Like, "green with envy"?

KYLE: That's a figure of speech.

CASSIA: Green: a metaphor for someone greedy and mean and for no reason at all keeping the green. . . .

KYLE: A metaphor for something deeper in life. You know, the green crayon, a metaphor for things we loved and things we lost and things that we never really appreciated until we could never have them back. Do you think you might learn something from this? Do you think, if you ever come across another green crayon again, that you'll appreciate it more, and hold on to it tighter, and use it first instead of leaving it for last? Do you think this might be a great big metaphor?

CASSIA: No. I think it's a green crayon.

KYLE: You're probably right.

CASSIA: I hate you.

KYLE: Why?

CASSIA: Because you're mean!

KYLE: You're the one yelling.

CASSIA: Okay. Okay. Please. Please can I please have the green crayon? I'll give you . . .

KYLE: You don't have anything I want.

CASSIA: I'll have the most beautiful picture I've ever drawn, and it will be beautiful and perfect, because of the green. And the green will be the most important thing, because your stupid metaphor will make me appreciate the green and use it perfectly. Not too much and not too little. And maybe you'll get yourself a metaphor of your own, of something that can only really truly happen once in the whole world, and it will be this picture, and I'll give it to you.

KYLE: You'll give me the picture? You sure you won't want the picture when it's done?

CASSIA: I'll still want it. But I'll give it to you.

[KYLE *hands* CASSIA *the green crayon.*]

KYLE: Green's my favorite color.

CASSIA: Mine too.

Happy Worst Day Ever

Arlene Hutton

Comic

CHRIS: 10 to 11
JACOB: 10 to 11

JACOB *and* CHRIS *are best friends, in the same 5th- or 6th-grade classroom.* JACOB*'s mom works in the lunchroom at* JACOB*'s school while his dad is overseas, serving in the military.* JACOB *is kind and studious, while* CHRIS, *in spite of having the best intentions, usually manages to mess things up and get into trouble. They are in the basement rec room at* JACOB*'s house. They are each blowing up a balloon.*

CHRIS: I want a cell phone.

JACOB: Why?

CHRIS: So I can call people.

JACOB: Who do you want to call?

CHRIS: Friends at school.

JACOB: You see them every day. You don't need a cell phone at school.

CHRIS: What if you got sick?

JACOB: I'd go see the nurse.

CHRIS: What if you got really sick and wanted to tell your mom?

JACOB: My mom works at the school.

CHRIS: Oh, yeah. [*They blow their balloons in silence.*] What if you wanted to call me?

JACOB: I don't have to call you. We hang out together.

CHRIS: Yeah. [CHRIS *blows the balloon.*] My mom likes it when I hang out with you.

JACOB: Is that why you do it?

CHRIS: My mom says you set a good example.

JACOB: Yeah. Everybody's mom likes me.

CHRIS: You never get in trouble. I always get in trouble.

JACOB: Don't do bad stuff.

CHRIS: I don't know it's bad until after I do it.

JACOB: Well, then, don't do it the next time.

CHRIS: I forget.

JACOB: [*With his balloon.*] There. Now tie it off.

[*They tie the ends of their balloons.*]

CHRIS: This is really how they make soccer balls?

JACOB: That's what my dad says.

CHRIS: Cool.

[JACOB *picks up two kitchen towels and hands one to* CHRIS.]

JACOB: Now wrap the towel around the balloon.

CHRIS: Are we gonna get in trouble?

JACOB: For what?

CHRIS: For taking your mom's towels.

JACOB: We'll put them back after.

CHRIS: Sometimes things are trouble one day and the next day it doesn't matter.

JACOB: Like what?

CHRIS: Like messy rooms.

JACOB: I like my room neat.

CHRIS: My room would be boring if it was neat.

JACOB: Now wrap the rubber bands around the balloon.

[*They attempt to keep the towels on the balloons with the rubber bands.*]

CHRIS: I'm gonna be in trouble when I get home.

JACOB: Why?

CHRIS: I didn't make my bed.

JACOB: Why not?

CHRIS: What's the point when you're just gonna get right back in it again.

JACOB: I make my bed every day. And I help my mom. And I promised to do my homework.

CHRIS: I promise stuff too, but then I forget that I promised.

JACOB: I never forget what I promised my dad.

CHRIS: But he's not even here.

JACOB: It doesn't matter. A promise is a promise. And when you make a promise you keep it. I promised you we'd make soccer balls, didn't I?

CHRIS: Yeah.

JACOB: And here's our soccer balls.

CHRIS: We could make a bigger ball if we had sheets. And if I took the sheet off my bed, I wouldn't have to make it anymore.

JACOB: You know what? When my dad comes home for good, I won't make my bed anymore. Why waste time making my bed when I can spend it with my dad?

CHRIS: Yeah.

[CHRIS *is still trying to finish making the ball.*]

JACOB: He'll walk with me to the bus stop. He'll wear his uniform! He'll help us with our science projects!

CHRIS: Science projects! Yeah! Wanna do something with mice?

JACOB: We'd get in trouble if we got real mice.

CHRIS: How do you always know what's trouble and what isn't trouble?

JACOB: Magnets would be cool.

CHRIS: Maggots? Yeah!

JACOB: Magnets.

CHRIS: How about cockroaches?

JACOB: Put stuff between two magnets and see if they still attract.

CHRIS: Something with cockroaches and magnets.

JACOB: Something with candles. Something scientific.

CHRIS: Do you have candles? We could catch cockroaches and see if they go towards the candles.

JACOB: My mom bought birthday candles.

CHRIS: [*Visualizing and thinking as hard as possible.*] Fill the balloons with water and hold them over the candles while the cockroaches are . . . [CHRIS *gestures while thinking this through, and then trails off.*]

JACOB: GPS.

CHRIS: Yeah! GPS. Put little GPS's on the cockroaches.

JACOB: Like little army vehicles.

CHRIS: My dad has GPS. He yells at it.

JACOB: My dad doesn't yell.

CHRIS: My dad yells at the GPS. And his computer. And the TV, when it's football.

JACOB: They get to watch football over there. And sometimes they play football. In the sand.

[JACOB *and* CHRIS *play with their homemade soccer balls.*]

CHRIS: That's cool.

JACOB: You don't want to get tackled. The ants bite you if you fall down in the sand.

CHRIS: Are there cockroaches?

JACOB: He didn't say anything about cockroaches.

CHRIS: Ask him about cockroaches. Call him up. Ask him about cockroaches.

JACOB: He doesn't get phone calls when he's on a mission.

CHRIS: Next time he calls, ask him about cockroaches.

JACOB: He can't call until his mission is over.

CHRIS: Yeah, his mission.

JACOB: Then he gets fifteen days leave. To come home.

CHRIS: Maybe he'll come home for your birthday.

JACOB: It's called "leave."

CHRIS: Maybe he'll leave in time to sing you "Happy Birthday" in person.

JACOB: [*Wistfully.*] He promised he would some day.

CHRIS: Where's the candles? Let's see how fast they melt when we blow on them.

JACOB: They're for my birthday party.

CHRIS: You're gonna have a birthday party?

JACOB: That's what my mom says. You can come.

CHRIS: Your mom's giving you a birthday party because your dad's coming home.

JACOB: He would tell me if he was coming home.

CHRIS: He wants to surprise you. Maybe it'll be on the news. Give me the candles.

JACOB: They're for my birthday.

CHRIS: There's more than enough here.

JACOB: I don't think we're supposed to.

CHRIS: It's for science.

Happy Worst Day Ever

Arlene Hutton

Seriocomic

GLORIE: 10 to 11
JACOB: 10 to 11

JACOB *and* GLORIE *are classmates, in the 5th or 6th grade, but they couldn't be more different.* JACOB, *an army brat, is bright, kind and generous, but a little awkward and nerdy.* GLORIE *is the most popular girl at school, very full of herself. She would rather watch TV than do her homework and is fascinated by a show called America's Singing Sensation. When* GLORIE *gets behind with her schoolwork, their teacher forces them to study together so* JACOB *can help her. Things are further complicated by the fact that their teacher has challenged* GLORIE *to stop using the word "like" in like every other sentence.* GLORIE *is sitting at a table in the school library, with a notebook open.* JACOB *enters and sits next to her. There is a long silence.*

GLORIE: You're late.

JACOB: Yeah.

[JACOB *takes out his books.*]

GLORIE: We have to study until—[*She starts to say "like" but catches herself.*] until one-thirty.

JACOB: Yeah.

GLORIE: Okay. I don't get this assignment. Why is this . . . a noun?

JACOB: You have to figure it out on your own.

GLORIE: You have to like help me. [*Correcting herself.*] You have to help me.

JACOB: No, I don't.

GLORIE: Ms. Adkins said you did.

JACOB: Ms. Adkins said I have to sit with you at this table in the library. She didn't say I had to help you today.

GLORIE: She said it was—It was time for us to study together.

JACOB: And we are studying together. We're sitting here at the same table. We're both studying. Or at least one of us is. Except when someone interrupts him.

GLORIE: I can't concentrate. I'm too sad.

JACOB: I don't care.

GLORIE: David Ying lost *American's Singing Sensation.*

JACOB: I really don't care.

GLORIE: How could he lose?

JACOB: You can't get everything you want.

GLORIE: Why not?

JACOB: Life doesn't work that way.

GLORIE: He was—he was the best.

JACOB: He didn't die. He just didn't win.

GLORIE: I wonder how he feels.

JACOB: He'll make a CD and you can listen to it all the time.

GLORIE: He looked so sad.

JACOB: I don't want to hear about David Sing anymore.

GLORIE: It's David Ying.

JACOB: I don't care.

GLORIE: You're in like—you're in a really bad mood today.

JACOB: So are you.

GLORIE: I have a good reason.

JACOB: So do I.

GLORIE: What's your reason?

JACOB: What's yours?

GLORIE: You first.

JACOB: You brought it up.

[*Silence.* **JACOB** *goes back to his studying.*]

GLORIE: [*Waiting as long as she can.*] I told you. David Ying lost.

JACOB: That's not a good enough reason. You don't even know him.

GLORIE: So . . . what's your big reason?

JACOB: Nothing.

GLORIE: I told you mine. You have to like—you have to tell me your reason.

[JACOB *is stoic.*]

JACOB: My dad didn't get to come home for my birthday.

GLORIE: Oh.

JACOB: I thought he was going to come and then he didn't.

GLORIE: See, you can't get everything you want.

JACOB: I study. I make my bed. I help with the dishes. I keep my promises. Why can't my dad come home?

GLORIE: Parents are weird.

JACOB: He didn't come. Again. My dad's never been there for my birthday. Not my whole life. And now the army's not even letting him come for Christmas. Again.

GLORIE: I don't get to spend birthdays with my dad, either. Not anymore. He gets Thanksgiving and Father's Day and, and, um, maybe something else, I forget. And every other weekend and a month in the summertime. My mom gets birthdays and Christmas.

JACOB: At least you get him every other weekend.

GLORIE: Someday your dad'll be home for good.

JACOB: Yeah.

GLORIE: Mine never will.

JACOB: I'm sorry.

[*Silence.*]

GLORIE: I'm sorry.

JACOB: Thanks. [*Silence.*] I miss my dad.

GLORIE: I miss my dad, too.

[*Silence.*]

JACOB: I got mad. I made my mom cry.

GLORIE: My mom cries a lot.

JACOB: What do you do when your mom cries?

GLORIE: I tell her I love her.

JACOB: Yeah. I should have done that. I'll do it when I get home. My mom said I could ride the bus home today.

GLORIE: That's cool.

JACOB: Yeah. When I get home I'm gonna tell her I love her.

GLORIE: It sometimes makes them cry when you tell them that, but it's okay. It like—it helps them.

JACOB: Yeah. I know what you mean. Sometimes crying is good.

GLORIE: I cried last night.

JACOB: Why?

GLORIE: Because David Ying lost.

JACOB: Didn't he come in second?

GLORIE: Yeah.

JACOB: So he didn't lose. He won. He won second place.

GLORIE: I wanted him to be the Singing Sensation.

JACOB: You know, it's the second-place winner who has the best career.

GLORIE: Really?

JACOB: Yeah. Because he has to work harder. He does better the next time.

[*A pause, as they ponder this.*]

GLORIE: Ms. Adkins says I'm doing better.

JACOB: She said that?

GLORIE: Yeah. She says she thinks I'll pass.

JACOB: That's great!

GLORIE: She said she could see me trying not to use that word.

JACOB: "Like"?

GLORIE: Don't say it!

JACOB: Like. Like. Like.

[*Each time he says the word, she reacts as if she were being tickled.*]

GLORIE: Don't!

JACOB: Like!

GLORIE: [*Having a fit of giggles.*] Stop it! [*He stops.*]

JACOB: So how much time do we have?

GLORIE: Until one-thirty.

JACOB: It's quarter past one.

GLORIE: We only have like five minutes?

JACOB: No. We have fifteen minutes.

GLORIE: But it's quarter past.

JACOB: Yeah.

GLORIE: So that's—that's twenty-five minutes after.

JACOB: No.

GLORIE: A quarter is twenty-five.

JACOB: No, a quarter is fifteen.

GLORIE: Duh. I know a quarter is like twenty-five cents.

JACOB: Yeah, but a quarter hour is fifteen minutes. A quarter means one-fourth. You divide by four. A dollar has one hundred cents, so a quarter of a dollar is twenty-five cents. That's why they call it a quarter. An hour is sixty minutes . . . [*He's drawing a clock on a piece of paper.*]

GLORIE: And if you divide sixty by four, it's fifteen. A fourth of an hour is fifteen minutes.

JACOB: Yes!

GLORIE: A fourth is a quarter is fifteen. So if it's one-fifteen, we have fifteen minutes until it's one-thirty.

JACOB: That's right.

GLORIE: Did I just do fractions?

JACOB: Yeah.

GLORIE: Oh. Fractions. So that's fractions.

[*They go back to work.*]

Have a Hoppy Holiday

Scot Walker

Comic

PAT: 9 to 12, a boy or a girl
CHRIS: 9 to 12, a boy or a girl

CHRIS *is in* PAT'S *house.* PAT *enters, crying.*

PAT: He's dead.

CHRIS: What?

PAT: He just croaked . . . right there before my eyes! He croaked!

CHRIS: Your dad? He was in the hospital . . . is he okay?

[PAT *falls onto the floor in a heap, banging fists.*]

PAT: One minute he was hopping all around the room, and now he's gone . . . like he hopped off to froggy paradise!

CHRIS: Oh my goodness! You mean Hoppy died!

PAT: What do you think I've been crying about? I bet Hoppy's eating a thousand heavenly bugs for breakfast right this very minute.

CHRIS: Shouldn't we get a . . . bag or something? Or . . . [*Voice fades off.*]

PAT: I guess. . . . But he probably needs a few minutes to stiffen up . . . I want to make sure he's really gone.

CHRIS: I think a box is better than a bag.

PAT: You're right. Hoppy would like that; it'll give him more room to play with his friends. But we've got to find a safe place for him.

CHRIS: Won't he be in Heaven?

PAT: I wonder what Heaven's really like . . . for a frog.

CHRIS: And what type of service we should give him.

PAT: Maybe we can ask Father O'Brien?

CHRIS: Maybe, but when Father blessed the animals, he didn't bless any frogs. Do you think Jesus even wants frogs in Heaven? Didn't we read about the plague of frogs back in the Bible—when Moses had them descend on the Egyptians? I bet God hates frogs!

PAT: Maybe Allah likes frogs? Do you think Hoppy might have been Muslim?

CHRIS: Maybe.

PAT: Or Hindu? I read the Hindus worship millions of gods—maybe one of them is a frog. Maybe Hoppy could be a Hindu god right now.

CHRIS: Or maybe Hoppy's just an atheist.

[Both children look up to Heaven for a moment, and then down.]

PAT: Maybe that's good news—if he didn't believe in it, then at least he won't go down there.

[Both children look up to heaven for a moment, and then down.]

Now we don't have to worry about Hoppy going up or down.

CHRIS: We can just bury him in the backyard so his friends can come and find him.

PAT: He'll be so happy outside next to the lily pads, it will be like he's having a Hoppy Holiday!

CHRIS: I've got an idea. . . . Excuse me.

[CHRIS exits. PAT walks to the window, looking up and up and up, turns, takes a deep breath.]

PAT: He'll be safe again, he'll be safe forever and ever.

[CHRIS returns with a small box containing HOPPY, takes PAT's hand, and slowly heads toward the door as they sing.]

CHRIS and **PAT:** *[Singing to any tune they devise.]* HOPPY was a bullfrog, he was a friend of mine . . .

CHRIS: Wait! Now that we know Hoppy was an atheist, we can give him all those good things Mom told us were bad for him. *[Reaching inside a pocket.]* Look, I've got a cookie.

PAT: *[Reaching in pocket.]* And I've got candy.

[*The children place the cookie and candy inside the box and begin to exit as they sing to whatever tune they make up.*]

CHRIS: Hoppy was a good old bullfrog . . .

PAT: He was a friend of mine . . .

CHRIS: Hoppy was my beautiful old bullfrog . . .

CHRIS and **PAT:** We'll love him all the time.

The House of Broken Dreams

Carol Costa

Dramatic

TRACEY: 15
JOE: 15

TRACEY *and* JOE *are sitting at the kitchen table having soft drinks.* TRACEY, *desperate to save her parents' marriage, enlists the help of her boyfriend,* JOE, *who is now having second thoughts and wants out of the deceitful plan.*

TRACEY: Do you want some chips or something to eat?

JOE: No thanks. I'm in training. I shouldn't even be drinking this.

TRACEY: [*Teasing.*] We do a lot of things we shouldn't do. [JOE *looks around nervously.*]

JOE: Maybe I'd better go. Your stepmother could come home any minute now.

TRACEY: She's not my stepmother. She's my father's mistress, but not for long. It's beginning to work.

JOE: Please, Tracey, I don't want to hear it. The less I know, the better I like it.

TRACEY: You promised to help me, and I'm not going to let you back out now. I've almost got her convinced, and when they confront you . . .

[JOE *jumps up nervously.*]

JOE: Confront me? You never said anything about that!

TRACEY: Well, of course they're going to confront you. That's what parents do in these situations.

[JOE *begins to walk around and* TRACEY *gets up to try and calm him down. She tries to put her arms around him, but he shrugs her off.*]

JOE: Leave me alone, Tracey. I want out of this. I can't handle the tension.

TRACEY: Well, you'd better learn. It's too late for you to back out now.

[*Now* JOE *looks terrified.*]

JOE: Oh, my God. You're not really pregnant?

[TRACEY *laughs.*]

TRACEY: Don't be so dumb. You can't get pregnant from just kissing boys.

JOE: Right. I know that, but saying you are when you're not is just as bad for me.

TRACEY: Oh for pete's sake, relax. I'm the one who'll be taking all the heat. I'll say I talked you into it. Does that make you feel better? [*She smiles and bats her eyes at him.*]

JOE: Cut it out, Tracey. You're driving me crazy.

TRACEY: You and Cynthia. She's a nervous wreck and I love it.

JOE: You know I never understood any of this. Why are you doing this, anyway?

TRACEY: We're convincing Cynthia that I'm pregnant. She'll tell my dad, and he and my mom will have to face their daughter's crisis together.

JOE: Okay . . . so how will that get rid of your dad's girlfriend? He'll still be in love with her instead of your mom.

TRACEY: He is not in love with that witch. He just thinks he is, because she tricked him into it. Once I get him and mom communicating again, he'll realize what a terrible mistake it was to leave her for Cynthia.

JOE: I don't know, Tracey. This whole thing could blow up in our faces. What if your father tries to kill me?

TRACEY: [*Laughing.*] Don't be silly. My father is much too civilized for physical violence. He's never even spanked me or Randy.

JOE: Maybe he should have.

TRACEY: Maybe we should rehearse what you're going to say when they confront you.

[Joe *jumps again.*]

JOE: Forget it, Tracey. I want out of this deal.

[Tracey *grabs him.*]

TRACEY: You're not backing out on me. I'm going to tell them you're the father of my baby. Come to think of it, you could deny it. That might make it more effective.

JOE: Oh my God. How did I get into this?

TRACEY: Seems to me you were perfectly willing to do anything I asked when I gave you the answers to the chemistry test.

JOE: Failing it would have gotten me kicked off the football team.

TRACEY: You got what you wanted. Now you're going to help me get what I want.

JOE: You caught me in a weak moment.

TRACEY: That's what I'll tell my dad. [*Very dramatically.*] He caught me in a weak moment. I felt so alone and unloved.

JOE: I'm a dead man.

TRACEY: Stop worrying. I told you my father doesn't believe in violence.

JOE: I think mine does.

TRACEY: I thought your parents were going to be in Europe for the next two months.

JOE: They are, but when they find out about the baby, they'll be back on the next plane to kill me . . . What am I saying? There is no baby!

[TRACEY *paces for a few seconds, thinking.*]

TRACEY: Look, before I let them call your parents, I'll tearfully confess that there were other boys, and I really don't know who the father is.

JOE: What other boys? I thought we were going steady.

TRACEY: Joe, try and concentrate. There are no other boys and there is no baby. It's all a plot to get rid of Cynthia.

JOE: I'd better leave. I don't want her to catch me here again.

TRACEY: Honestly, Joe—how could I be having a baby if I don't spend time with boys? Anyway, she's out on one of her secret missions again. Wouldn't it be funny if she had another boyfriend, and was planning on dumping my dad anyway?

JOE: You think that's possible?

TRACEY: I don't know. But whenever she goes out like this, she's always very nice to me when she comes back, until I get her upset again.

JOE: How can you be so mean, Tracey?

TRACEY: She broke up my home . . . she deserves to suffer.

JOE: I have to get home. I've got an exam tomorrow. You're not going to drop the bomb tonight are you? I really need to study. I hope you're not dropping the bomb tonight.

TRACEY: Don't worry. My mom isn't coming for a few more days. I want to wait until just before she gets here.

In a Garden

Martha Patterson

Seriocomic

STEVIE: 7 to 10, a boy
TOMASINA: 7 to 10, a girl
FLORA: 7 to 10, a girl

STEVIE *and* TOMASINA *are sitting on a wall.* TOMASINA *is holding a rose.* TOMASINA *has a pair of homemade stilts lying next to her.* STEVIE *has a small knapsack.*

STEVIE: Give me that rose.

TOMASINA: No way.

STEVIE: I said, give me that rose.

TOMASINA: [*Smelling the rose.*] What do you want with a rose?

STEVIE: I want it to give to Flora.

TOMASINA: Flora. What a pretty name. And you like Flora, do you?

STEVIE: I'm not telling you my secrets.

TOMASINA: But you already have! You want to give this rose to Flora.

STEVIE: Maybe I do.

TOMASINA: You can pick another one.

STEVIE: But they have thorns!

TOMASINA: I almost pricked my finger picking this one.

STEVIE: Give it to me.

TOMASINA: I won't!

STEVIE: You're not very nice, Tomasina.

TOMASINA: Why do you like Flora so much? I get better grades in school, and I have long hair, and even though my hair isn't curly like hers, it's down to my waist!

STEVIE: She's nice to me.

TOMASINA: In what way, may I ask?

STEVIE: She gave me half her peanut butter sandwich yesterday, when I accidentally dropped my lunch into the pond.

TOMASINA: Then I'll give you half my sandwich. [*She pulls half a sandwich from her lunch bag.*] Here. Peanut butter.

STEVIE: Thank you. [*He takes a bite.*]

TOMASINA: With the best kind of jelly—grape, that my mother made!

STEVIE: Mmph!! Thank you, Tomasina! [FLORA *enters, skipping rope.*] Flora!

TOMASINA: Dimwit.

FLORA: [*She stops skipping rope.*] What did you call me?

TOMASINA: Nothing.

STEVIE: [*Still chewing the sandwich.*] Mmph!! I wanted to give you a flower, Flora—but Tomasina won't let me have hers.

FLORA: She's a little witch. She doesn't like me at all.

TOMASINA: He only likes you because you're the cutest girl in school.

FLORA: I know how you feel about me. Besides, your parents are divorced. Mine aren't. [*To* STEVIE.] Which of these pretty flowers were you going to give me?

STEVIE: The sunflower—the long one, with the big yellow petals—but it's too big to pick.

FLORA: I don't like that one.

STEVIE: I also tried to pick you a rose, but I pricked my finger.

FLORA: Wuss. [*Smiles to herself and sits down.*]

TOMASINA: [*To* STEVIE.] I'll give you my rose to give to Flora after all.

[*Hands it to him.*] But she doesn't like you, you know.

STEVIE: [*Handing* FLORA *the rose.*] Will you be my girlfriend?

FLORA: [*Still smiling.*] I won't! I like David.

STEVIE: But I'm giving you a rose!

FLORA: I'm lucky. *All* the boys like me!

TOMASINA: See what I mean? She's a little witch.

FLORA: My mother says I'll break a lot of hearts someday.

STEVIE: You've already broken mine.

FLORA: She says I have eyes like cornflowers.

TOMASINA: Stevie, I'm not hungry. Would you like the other half of my sandwich? [*Hands it, wrapped in a baggie, to* STEVIE.]

STEVIE: [*Putting the half a sandwich into his knapsack.*] Thank you.

TOMASINA: And would you like to walk on my stilts? My stepfather made them for me to play on. It's easy! You just step up on the little footrests and walk! [*Shows him the stilts.*]

STEVIE: Thank you! [*Gets up on the stilts and walks around.*]

FLORA: You look like an idiot.

STEVIE: I do not!

TOMASINA: You can play with them as much as you like!

STEVIE: This is a blast!

FLORA: [*To* TOMASINA.] You'll do anything to get a boy.

TOMASINA: I know how to be nice.

FLORA: I got an A on the spelling test. You only got a C, even though you're supposed to be smart.

STEVIE: [*Getting off the stilts and giving them back to* TOMASINA.] Tomasina is smart at math.

FLORA: So?

STEVIE: So, she can help me with a subject I'm not good at.

FLORA: [*Shaking her curls.*] I'll never let you kiss me.

STEVIE: I don't think I want to kiss you. Tomasina is my friend now, not you.

TOMASINA: [*To* STEVIE.] Would you like to pick some more flowers with me?

STEVIE: No. I want to go home and build a model airplane. I got a kit for my birthday.

FLORA: Boring!

TOMASINA: That sounds like fun! Can I go home with you?

STEVIE: Sure can. And as for you, Flora, you can have all the roses in this garden, but I like Tomasina better!

TOMASINA: [*To* FLORA.] See? It pays to be nice.

FLORA: [*Sticks her tongue out at* TOMASINA.] I have an iPod.

STEVIE: Big whoop.

FLORA: Who needs flowers, anyway? [*She kicks the pair of stilts that are lying on the ground.*]

Who needs either one of you? [*She exits.*]

STEVIE: [*Taking* TOMASINA's *hand.*] Come on! I'll show you how to make sure the airplane glue doesn't get stuck to your fingers.

[*He kisses her on the cheek and picks up his knapsack. She picks up her stilts. He takes them from her to carry, and they exit.*]

I Went There

Jenny Lyn Bader

Originally written for *You Are Now the Owner
of This Suitcase*, a collaboratively authored,
multiwriter play directed and developed by
Ari Laura Kreith at Theatre 167.

Dramatic

RUBY ROO: 9, a girl
4: 9, a boy

You Are Now the Owner of This Suitcase *is a play set in
magical Jackson Heights—a Queens, New York, neighborhood
known for its cultural diversity—and inspired by the fairytales
and folktales of the cultures of that neighborhood. At the end of
act 1, the girl* RUBY ROO *comes to life in a moment of
enchantment. The scene "I Went There" takes place at the
beginning of act 2 on the eve of* RUBY ROO's *10th birthday. She
has become friendly with a boy known only as "4," who lives on
the streets.*

RUBY ROO: You went there? I don't believe you.

4: I was looking for cans.

RUBY ROO: Cans?

4: Soda cans. I return them for nickels. I've always found a lot of soda cans. Until the cold weather set in this year. And suddenly—no soda cans. Anywhere I could see. But I heard there might be some there.

RUBY ROO: Uh-huh, but didn't you also hear that there's a witch there? And that you could drown there? And that people go in there and never come back? Or come back completely unrecognizable?

4: I heard there were soda cans.

RUBY ROO: Yuh-huh.

4: I needed the nickels for a new pair of shoes. My feet were hurting.

RUBY ROO: But you never heard about no magic.

4: Sure, maybe people said it was spooky, it was magic, it was haunted. It sounds familiar. But really—I need those cans. I go there . . . [*They begin to reenact the scene; 4 brings* RUBY ROO *along.*] . . . and there they are. But some of the sodas . . . they're not what you expect.

RUBY ROO: What do you mean? Like Mountain Dew?

4: Like, I don't know. Not that. Slice. Orange Cream. Sodas I never even heard of. With funny designs. Brilliant rainbow soda cans. I bundled them up in a blue bag.

[4 *bundles the sodas in a blue bag. It starts making funny sounds.*]

RUBY ROO: I don't like this. Let's get outta here!

4: You're not here. I'm just telling you about it.

Ruby Roo: You're telling it too well. Because I can see it. Weird cans. A bag . . .

4: And there was this strange sound.

Ruby Roo: Yes, that!

[*Strange clinking and music.*]

4: The cans knocked together and they . . .

Ruby Roo and **4:** . . . played music!

4: Then that lady with the funny hat who lives next door came out. [Ruby Roo *screams.*] Why are you screaming?

Ruby Roo: She scares me.

4: Why?

Ruby Roo: I don't know.

4: She asked me for a story. I told her, "Lady, I'm not a storyteller."

Ruby Roo: What do you mean, you're not a storyteller? Aren't you telling a story now?

4: Yes now. But then—I had no story. That's part of the story. Part of the story is me getting a story. See I wasn't a storyteller. And I wasn't a doctor, either . . .

Ruby Roo: A doctor?

4: But suddenly there was a funeral procession, with three men holding a gigantic turquoise coffin—and they said, this is the distinguished doctor Christian Valiutis.

RUBY ROO: Which is not your name.

4: Which is not my name. But suddenly it was, too. It wasn't and it was. They said one of the men in the funeral procession was so tall, they were holding the coffin lopsidedly, and if I were that distinguished doctor could I shorten this man's legs.

RUBY ROO: What did you do?

4: I cut his legs off. And put them together again.

RUBY ROO: I don't like this story. First the witch . . .

4: She's not a witch, she's a next-door neighbor who looks like a witch.

RUBY ROO: Now the amputation.

4: I'm telling you his foot just went into his leg at a new place, and became like new. I suddenly knew how to be a doctor. And then I went into this little bar . . .

RUBY ROO: [*Alarmed.*] Did you get carded?

4: They just asked me to play the ukulele.

RUBY ROO: Did you tell them, no, you were a famous surgeon?

4: I played the ukulele.

RUBY ROO: Get out of here, it's getting creepy!

4: And then a woman walked up to me and said she needed something translated into Chinese.

RUBY ROO: Which you don't speak. Except you do.

4: Everything arrived at that moment. *Cun bu nan shang xin!* [*Translation: It was magic!*]

RUBY ROO: Do you speak Chinese now?

4: *Ni zhe dao.* [*Translation: You know it.*]

RUBY ROO: What did she want translated?

4: A love letter.

RUBY ROO: Did you translate it?

4: And delivered it. They're married now.

RUBY ROO: What did you do with the soda cans?

4: I realized I had become another person and I ran very, very far from the soda cans.

RUBY ROO: To . . .

4: The electronics store. On the corner of 78th, the Babelware electronic store. I read the sign in the window.

RUBY ROO: Which sign?

4: It says "Languages Spoken Here: English Spanish Mandarin Korean Hindi Russian Ukrainian German Greek Turkish Ravenish".

RUBY ROO: Ravenish?

4: The language of ravens. Ever since coming out of that forbidden alleyway, I understand Ravenish, and Pyelanguage, and all of the languages of the birds. And now here there must be another human speaking Ravenish.

RUBY ROO: And did you go in?

4: Go in where?

RUBY ROO: To the electronics store!

4: Of course not! That would be scary.

RUBY ROO: No. You've been to the forbidden place now. Now you can do anything. You have to go!!

Judy Maccabee

Susan Horowitz

Dramatic

JONATHAN: 12
JUDY: 12

The setting is Jerusalem, 165 BCE (the origin of Hanukkah).
JUDY, *disguised as a boy, is secretly in love with* JONATHAN, *the nephew of Judah Maccabee.* JONATHAN *writes on a scroll and gives it to* JUDY, *who looks at it upside down and pretends to read.* JONATHAN *turns the scroll around.*

JONATHAN: So you can't read. Why do you try to fake it?

JUDY: I can read . . . Oh, all right, I can't. But I'm not dumb.

JONATHAN: I never said you were. Do you want me to teach you to read?

JUDY: It's hard, right?

JONATHAN: Nothing important comes easy—like freedom. But it's worth fighting for. Reading is freedom, too.

JUDY: I'm free. I go where I want. Do what I want. I know more than you do about surviving in the street.

JONATHAN: There's more to life than the street.

JUDY: Like what?

JONATHAN: Like knowledge, new ideas, and . . . poetry.

JUDY: Poetry?!

JONATHAN: Yeah.

JUDY: You read poetry?

JONATHAN: I write it, too. Someday, I'll show my poetry to my soul mate.

JUDY: Your what?

JONATHAN: Don't you believe in soul mates?

JUDY: Soul what?

JONATHAN: [*Drawing closer.*] Two people who are meant to be together—forever.

JUDY: Really . . . ? Uh, I mean . . . What else is reading good for?

JONATHAN: Directions. If you could read, you could find Bathsheba's house.

JUDY: Market, over the bridge, then left.

JONATHAN: How do you know?

JUDY: She leaves the market by the bridge. The big houses are on the left.

JONATHAN: How do you know she lives in a big house?

JUDY: By the way she talks.

JONATHAN: You talked to Bathsheba?

JUDY: What's so strange about that?

JONATHAN: A nice girl doesn't talk to boys.

JUDY: You better get your nose out of a book.

JONATHAN: You better not disrespect Bathsheba.

JUDY: What do you care?

JONATHAN: She's my fiancée. My future wife.

JUDY: Your what?!

JONATHAN: We've been engaged ever since we were babies. Of course, she never speaks to me because nice girls don't speak to boys.

JUDY: But you still want to marry her?

JONATHAN: She'll be my wife. She'll cook for me and do . . . what wives do. It's not like we'll talk.

JUDY: Don't you want to marry someone you can talk to?

JONATHAN: You can't talk to girls. If I need to talk, I'll talk to you. David and Jonathan—best friends forever—like in the Torah. Now tell me your secret.

JUDY: What secret?

JONATHAN: I told you about writing poetry. Now you tell me your secret.

JUDY: I—I don't have any secrets. I'm boring . . . and I'm in a hurry! I have to guard Bathsheba—your soul mate.

[JUDY *runs out.*]

Le Morte d'Alex

Brandon M. Crose

Seriocomic

ALEXIS: 13 to 15, a teenage girl
CHRIS: 13 to 15, a teenage boy

*ALEXIS arrives home after school with her new boyfriend,
CHRIS, who wants to do things with ALEXIS but is less eager to
tell his friends that they are dating. The setting is a living room.
ALEXIS enters, followed by CHRIS. They both have their school
bags.*

ALEXIS: Howie . . . ? Are you home? [*Beat.*] Nope! All
alone.

CHRIS: When does he usually come home?

ALEXIS: Depends. Whenever he wants, since he made
assistant manager.

CHRIS: Great.

ALEXIS: What's wrong?

CHRIS: Nothing. I just don't think he likes me.

ALEXIS: I think he thinks that you don't like me.

CHRIS: You know that I like you.

ALEXIS: Do your friends know that you like me?

CHRIS: My friends are stupid. Forget about them.

ALEXIS: Why would you want to be friends with stupid people?

CHRIS: They're not always stupid. Just sometimes.

ALEXIS: That's a relief.

CHRIS: Are we going to make out, or what?

ALEXIS: Be still, my heart!

CHRIS: You know what I mean.

ALEXIS: Yes. You mean, "Are we going to make out, or what?"

CHRIS: Well, are we?

ALEXIS: I dunno.

CHRIS: Do you want to make out?

ALEXIS: You gave me chapped lips last time.

CHRIS: C'mon, before your uncle comes home.

ALEXIS: You also tried to put your hand up my shirt.

CHRIS: That's what people *do* when they make out.

ALEXIS: What people?

CHRIS: *People*. Everyone.

ALEXIS: Not you and me.

CHRIS: Not yet.

ALEXIS: Swine.

CHRIS: You know I like you a lot.

ALEXIS: How much?

CHRIS: This much.

[*He kisses her, then again, then harder.* ALEXIS *pushes him away.*]

ALEXIS: Ow!

CHRIS: What?

ALEXIS: You bit my lip!

CHRIS: You didn't like it?

ALEXIS: No!

CHRIS: Oh. Sorry.

ALEXIS: You're not very good at this.

CHRIS: Maybe I need more practice.

ALEXIS: Just go slow.

[*They begin to kiss again. It is awkward at first, then less awkward, but never comfortable.* CHRIS *moves* ALEXIS *to the couch. They fall onto it, still kissing.* CHRIS *starts to put his hand up* ALEXIS's *shirt.*]

ALEXIS: Stop that.

CHRIS: Stop what?

[ALEXIS *removes his hand. They continue kissing.* CHRIS *tries again to put his hand up her shirt.*]

ALEXIS: *Chris!*

CHRIS: It's okay! Just relax!

ALEXIS: It's not okay!

CHRIS: Fine!

[*They part. Awkward beat.*]

ALEXIS: Are you angry?

CHRIS: [*Is angry.*] No.

ALEXIS: I'm sorry.

CHRIS: If you were really sorry, you'd let me do it.

ALEXIS: That doesn't make any kind of sense at all.

CHRIS: Don't you like me?

ALEXIS: How could I not? You were the first person who called me a retard to my face. I knew it was love.

CHRIS: How many times do I have to apologize for that?

ALEXIS: You don't have to. I just like to hear it.

CHRIS: I'm sorry that I called you a retard.

ALEXIS: A *bleeping* retard.

CHRIS: I didn't say "bleeping."

ALEXIS: No, you did not!

CHRIS: Well, okay, you were sort of running around with a plastic sword, yelling things at no one.

ALEXIS: You were wearing an oversized hoodie and shoes that were two sizes too big for your feet.

CHRIS: That's what was in style.

ALEXIS: Plastic swords will always be in style.

CHRIS: You're better now.

ALEXIS: Yeah?

CHRIS: Yeah. A lot better . . .

[**CHRIS** *kisses her, and they lay back down on the couch. He begins inching his hand up her shirt.* **ALEXIS** *looks uncomfortable, but says nothing.*]

Letters to Sala

Arlene Hutton

Dramatic

ZUSI: 12 to 15
GUCIA: 12 to 15
SALA: 12 to 15
RACHEL: 12 to 15

In October of 1940, SALA GARNCARZ, a Jewish teen in Sosnowiec, Poland, left her home and family and reported to a Nazi labor camp, volunteering to go in the place of her older sister. Although SALA was told she would work for only 6 weeks and be paid, she spent the next 5 years in seven different slave labor camps, in Poland, Germany, and Czechoslovakia. She received over 300 pieces of mail, which she managed to hide. Over 40 years later she gave these letters to her daughter and granddaughters and they are now in the archives of the New York Public Library. The play tracks SALA's story as a teenager during the Holocaust and in New York City more than half a century later.

Schatzlar Labor Camp, Czechoslovakia, in May of 1945. SALA is on stage, reading a letter that is so old and frequently read that it is nearly falling apart. Pieces of paper are everywhere. SALA looks at the papers in amazement. SALA hears voices from offstage and quickly puts the letter in her pocket. ZUSI, GUCIA, *and* RACHEL *enter, excitedly. The lines overlap.*

ZUSI: Look! Look! Look!

GUCIA: They're everywhere!

SALA: What is it?

RACHEL: Don't touch them. Don't pick them up.

ZUSI: [*Pointing.*] There's the plane.

RACHEL: Are they going to bomb us?

SALA: Where's the plane?

GUCIA: Whose plane is it?

ZUSI: It's in the clouds. I can't see.

SALA: What do the papers say?

RACHEL: Don't touch them.

GUCIA: Maybe the war is over.

RACHEL: Maybe it's a trap.

SALA: How will we know?

RACHEL: Don't pick it up.

GUCIA: I can almost read it.

ZUSI: Do you think it's . . .

RACHEL: Is that a guard coming?

[*They all freeze.*]

SALA: I don't hear anything.

GUCIA: I don't hear . . .

SALA: I don't hear anything. It's completely quiet.

[*A long pause, while they listen.*]

GUCIA: It's too quiet.

SALA: It's never been this quiet.

ZUSI: I'm going to pick one up.

RACHEL: Don't pick it up. Just look at it. Don't touch it.

SALA: I'll watch out for the guard.

GUCIA: No. No! It is!

ZUSI: My God. My God!

SALA: [*Leaning over to read one herself.*] What?

RACHEL: What?

GUCIA: It's over.

[*They pick up some of the leaflets and read them.*]

ZUSI: [*Reading.*] Liberation.

SALA: What?

ZUSI: The war is over. That's what it says.

GUCIA: Germany has surrendered.

[RACHEL *begins crying hysterically.*]

ZUSI: Germany has surrendered!

SALA: It's over?

GUCIA: It's over! It's over!

SALA: Can we believe it?

[*They yell towards offstage, announcing the news.*]

GUCIA: The war is over!

ZUSI: [*Overlapping.*] The war is over!

SALA: [*Overlapping.*] The war is over!

RACHEL: [*Overlapping, still crying*] The war is over!

GUCIA: [*Overlapping.*] It's over!

ZUSI: [*Overlapping.*] The war is over!

[GUCIA *and* ZUSI *grab* RACHEL *and gleefully run offstage, laughing and crying. We hear them relaying the news offstage.* SALA *reaches into her pocket and pulls out her letter from home. She speaks to it.*]

SALA: What do we do now?

[*She runs off after the others.*]

Like Forever

Merridith Allen

Dramatic

CASEY: 15
SARAH: 15

CASEY *and* SARAH *have been best friends since kindergarten. In this flashback scene, the two girls are both 15 years old. They are waiting for a funeral service for* CASEY's *mother to begin.* CASEY *and* SARAH *sit together on a bench. They wear extremely inappropriate clothing for a funeral. Too sexy, or revealing, or brightly colored.* SARAH *holds a pen and guest book on her lap.*

CASEY: [*Indicating the guest book.*] Thanks for uh . . .

SARAH: Totally. I mean, like . . . least I can do.

CASEY: She said, like, all the time, when she had me, there must've been two babies instead of one, and the other somehow got misplaced . . . [SARAH *lights a cigarette. They sit in silence a moment.*] You can't smoke here.

SARAH: Why, cause it's a health hazard?

CASEY: My mom hated it that you smoke. [*Pause.* SARAH *takes a long drag off the cigarette.*]

SARAH: Where's your dad?

CASEY: I don't fuckin' know. Parking. Or drinking. Maybe both.

SARAH: Your brother?

CASEY: Drinking. Definitely drinking.

SARAH: They say anything about your dress?

CASEY: Fuck no! This was Mom's favorite. She got it in Miami I think.

SARAH: I could totally see that. I mean, I think it's hot, but . . .

CASEY: You really think Mom gives a shit what I'm wearing? I don't.

SARAH: Whatever. Just saying . . .

CASEY: Like that dress is so much better?

SARAH: [*Checking herself out.*] Hello—I'm wearing black.

CASEY: Yeah, but, seriously, that skirt . . .

SARAH: What the fuck—I've never been to a funeral before—I don't know what—hey, if you can wear that . . .

CASEY: Oh my God, forget it, okay? Like—I don't care. I just—I don't want to sit here, not saying anything, waiting for . . .

SARAH: Is she—I mean, have you seen her? Since . . .

CASEY: She looks . . . really pretty. I gave them my pink lip gloss. She used to borrow it all the time, so . . . [*Pause.*] Sarah? How am I going to . . . how am I supposed to walk up to her, with all these people all over, and kiss her good-bye? I think I'm going to totally lose my shit.

SARAH: I can walk with you.

CASEY: But you're going to lose your shit too.

SARAH: So? [*Pause.*]

CASEY: Can I tell you a secret?

SARAH: Yeah.

CASEY: I'm pissed at her.

SARAH: Why?

CASEY: Because she gave up.

SARAH: Case, wasn't she like, the last stage, or something . . .

CASEY: She had a choice. Six months ago. She had a choice. If she wanted to keep . . . or if she wouldn't, and she just . . . she gave up. And I have to walk down an aisle today—and my brother's gonna smell like gin and my dad's gonna reek of whiskey, and I have to kiss mom on the cheek and tell her good-bye and pretend like I'm sad because she's gone, and I'm not. I'm not sad. I'm fuckin' pissed.

[*Pause.*]

SARAH: But . . . how would you know—I mean, would it have mattered? If she kept going . . .

CASEY: I don't! But . . . I don't know, I don't understand, I just—I want her. I'm an asshole, right? Like, she was sick, I don't know—how much it hurt—I mean, because—and I still want her. I put this dress on last night—I slept in it, 'cause it still smells like her—she'll never talk to me again—I'll never hear her voice again—who's gonna call me Casey-loo again, huh? Nobody! It's bullshit! [*Pause.*]

SARAH: Yeah . . . it is . . .

Love Is a
Seven-Letter Word

Susan M. Steadman

Seriocomic

DONNA: 13
BOBBIE: 13
LAURIE: 14

Lights go up on a lovely September afternoon in the park.
DONNA, BOBBIE, *and* LAURIE *enter, carrying textbooks. They
settle down on a bench.*

DONNA: Did he answer your letter yet?

BOBBIE: Not yet.

LAURIE: You could call him, you know.

BOBBIE: I . . . I don't . . . I can't . . . oh . . . .

LAURIE: [*Teasing.*] Donna and I could call him for you.

DONNA: [*Pretending she's dialing a phone.*] Hello. May I
speak to Mark? Hello, Mark. I'm a friend of Bobbie—you
know, that pretty, sweet, smart girl you met at Rockaway
last summer?

LAURIE: [*Also pretending to speak on the phone.*] The sexy and sophisticated one. [*To* BOBBIE.] I'm on the kitchen extension. [*On the phone, again.*] Don't let her cool exterior fool you. She's really pining for your body.

BOBBIE: [*Protesting, though she's laughing.*] Laurie!

LAURIE: Yes, that's right . . . the one who kept beating you at Scrabble.

DONNA: Poor girl. Her mother never told her you're supposed to let the boy win, even if he's not as smart as you are.

LAURIE: Her mother also neglected to tell her that if he doesn't kiss you first, you should take the initiative.

DONNA: [*Placing her hand over the imaginary receiver.*] Hey! My mother never told me that.

LAURIE: [*Doing the same.*] Neither did mine, Donna. Fake it.

DONNA: [*On the telephone, again.*] Well, did you get her letter or not?

LAURIE: Oh, you got her letter, but you were so overcome with emotion you just didn't know how to answer it?

BOBBIE: Enough! People are looking at us.

LAURIE: Oh, good—let 'em look.

DONNA: Yeah, they'll be staring soon enough if we pledge Sigma Kap and have to wear those stupid little beanies and our blouses inside out.

BOBBIE: Donna, I'm not sure . . .

DONNA: At least it's just a short pledge period—then you're in.

LAURIE: Yeah. And Sigma Kap meets with all the best fraternities. Sometimes even college guys.

DONNA: College. My mother'll kill me.

LAURIE: Look, we won't be fourteen forever. In fact, I'll be fifteen next month.

BOBBIE: I'm thirteen.

LAURIE: Good grief, I keep forgetting you're still a baby.

BOBBIE: [*Irritated.*] Hardly.

DONNA: Don't mind Laurie.

LAURIE: [*To* BOBBIE, *grandly.*] Your youth is more than compensated for by your fortuitous family connections.

BOBBIE: Excuse me?

LAURIE: Your brother. Remember him? City College. T.E.P. fraternity. Is it coming back to you? [*To* DONNA, *in a bad German accent.*] Nurse, this is the worst case of amnesia I've seen in years. We may have to operate.

DONNA: [*Flirtatiously.*] Yes, Doctor. And we all know you're the best operator.

[*They all laugh.*]

BOBBIE: No, seriously. I'm having second thoughts about pledging. That is, providing I'm asked.

DONNA: You will be.

LAURIE: Yeah. They want all three of us. The Three Musketeers.

DONNA: In those beanies, we'll look like the Three Mouseketeers!

BOBBIE: Sororities are so . . . I don't know. Elitist. But not in a good way. No, no, not elitist. Uhm . . . exclusionist.

LAURIE: Come off it, Bobbie. All the school officers are in fraternities or sororities. All the most popular juniors and seniors. Even my history teacher was in a sorority when she went here.

DONNA: Miss Greenfield? [*She imitates a nearsighted woman with a waddle.*] "And now class, you will take out your text books and read pages 236 to 329 while I get a load off my feet, sneak a piece of chocolate, and pretend to be grading your homework."

BOBBIE: Seriously, even if I decide not to join Sigma Kap, we'll still be friends, won't we?

LAURIE: Of course. But let's be realistic. We won't be spending anywhere near as much time together.

DONNA: We'll still have homeroom together. And you'll see Laurie in honors English. But I'm afraid she's right. It won't be the same.

LAURIE: Unless you'd like to fix me up with your brother. Now, if I became, like, part of your family . . .

BOBBIE: He's taken, remember?

LAURIE: The good ones go fast.

Lunch Money

Jack Neary

Comic

TIMMY: 12 to 14
SUZANNE: 12 to 14

A schoolyard meanie is accused of stealing the lunch money from one of his classmates. In the classroom, a trial is held. SUZANNE, a middle schooler for the prosecution, questions TIMMY, another classmate, about the incident. TIMMY walks in and points to the witness chair.

TIMMY: Uh . . . Here? . . . Should I sit here?

SUZANNE: Yes! [TIMMY *starts to sit.*] NOT YET! [TIMMY *freezes.*] You have to swear first.

TIMMY: Oh. I never swear. My mother would ground me.

SUZANNE: No, no. Not that kind of swear. Raise your right hand.

[*He does.*]

TIMMY: Like this?

SUZANNE: Do you swear to tell the truth, the whole truth, and nothing but the truth?

TIMMY: So . . . let me get this straight . . . I'm swearing . . . without really swearing?

SUZANNE: Yes. Say "I do."

TIMMY: I do?

SUZANNE: Yes.

TIMMY: Yes what?

SUZANNE: You say "I do."

TIMMY: I do?

SUZANNE: Yes.

TIMMY: Yes what?

SUZANNE: JUST SAY "I DO!"

TIMMY: I DO!

SUZANNE: SIT! [TIMMY *sits.*] State your full name for the jury, please.

TIMMY: Timothy Thomas Timmons.

SUZANNE: [*Approaching* TIMMY.] Thank you. Mr. Timmons, would you please tell the court where you were at 11:31 in the morning on September 21st of this year?

TIMMY: Yes.

SUZANNE: Yes, what?

TIMMY: Yes, I will tell the court where I was at 11:31 in the morning on Septem . . .

SUZANNE: So tell!

TIMMY: Well . . . I was walking on the third floor of the school, past the lockers, on my way to history class.

SUZANNE: But . . . Mr. Timmons . . . 11:31 . . . doesn't that mean you were . . . late for history class?

TIMMY: Yes, it does. But I had a hall pass and . . .

SUZANNE: And doesn't that also mean that the hall was . . . empty at that time?

TIMMY: Yes, it does. Except for me. And one other person. But I had a hall pass and . . .

SUZANNE: One other person. Did you say, one other person, Mr. Timmons?

TIMMY: Yes. One other person. Plus me. Two of us. Me and one other person. Total of two. Persons.

SUZANNE: And would you describe that one other person for the court, Mr. Timmons?

TIMMY: Yes.

SUZANNE: Yes, what?

TIMMY: Yes, I will describe that one other person for the court . . .

SUZANNE: So describe!

TIMMY: It was Harlan Parmenter.

SUZANNE: That's . . . your description?

TIMMY: Yes. I figure the best way to describe him would be to tell you who he was and then you could just look at him sitting over there. [*Points.*]

SUZANNE: And what was Mr. Parmenter doing on the third-floor hallway by the lockers at 11:31 in the morning of September 21st of this year when he was supposed to be in class and the hallway was supposed to be completely empty?

TIMMY: Except for me.

SUZANNE: Mr. Timmons . . .

TIMMY: Because I had a hall pass . . .

SUZANNE: What was Harlan doing, Mr. Timmons?

TIMMY: [*Elaborately illustrating as he describes.*] He was prying open Mikey McDougald's locker and ripping open an envelope and taking money out of the envelope and putting the money in his pocket and putting the ripped envelope back in the locker and then shutting the locker and then walking away.

SUZANNE: And did Mr. Parmenter acknowledge your presence?

TIMMY: Excuse me?

SUZANNE: Did Mr. Parmenter . . . see you in the hallway?

TIMMY: Oh. Yes.

SUZANNE: And did he say anything to you?

TIMMY: Yes. He said, "If you tell anybody I did this, I will stuff you in a large Hefty bag and put you up for auction on eBay."

SUZANNE: [*Smiling.*] Thank you, Mr. Timmons. [*To TIMMY's unseen "defense attorney."*] Your witness!

A Masqued Proposal

Eric Scott Liberman

Dramatic

ZACH: 10, a boy
CASEY: 10, a girl

It's 1974. What appears to be the deal of her lifetime for 10-year-old CASEY BROOKS *could end up being a nasty con game conjured up by a reasonably roguish member of a narrowly known secret society, in the Washington, DC, area, dedicated to the preservation of all things Edgar Allan Poe. If* CASEY *is to succeed, she must use all her wits and the assistance of her best friend, 10-year-old* ZACHARY RODGERS, *to understand the meaning of Poe's verses, so she can win $5,000, as well as what her late father—a past society member himself—meant for her to gain . . . or to lose.*

ZACH: Five thousand dollars! We could all attend that music competition in England with that kind of money.

CASEY: I could give it to my mother so we can eat health foods from now on.

ZACH: Do you have that magazine?

CASEY: It's in my family's safety deposit box, sealed in a Mylar plastic envelope . . . [*She stands, and then places the letter in its envelope.*] . . . to keep it from falling apart. The darn thing is almost 150 years old. About the only thing my father left me.

ZACH: What about that silver clarinet?

CASEY: Yeah, that too.

ZACH: I didn't know your dad was dead . . . I thought he was just lost in Vietnam—somewhere.

CASEY: The army still thinks he's missing, but my mother thinks it's been too long.

ZACH: Why did he go anyway—I mean, the army doesn't really use poets, do they?

CASEY: I don't know—my uncle told me that he and my dad both signed up for the Special Services: where you go to entertain the soldiers with music . . .

ZACH: And read them poetry.

CASEY: I suppose. Anyway, my dad accidentally checked the box for Special Forces.

ZACH: What's that?

CASEY: Some exclusive group in the army.

ZACH: Like the Raven Society—was your dad in that, too?

CASEY: I don't know.

ZACH: Do you even know what they are? The Raven Society. They sound pretty creepy.

CASEY: Yes, I do know—they're a bunch of Edgar Allan Poe nuts like the crazies that sit around and talk about Sherlock Holmes all day—the Baker Street Irregulars.

ZACH: Who are the Baker Street Irregulars?

CASEY: The weirdos that sit around and talk about Sherlock Holmes all day.

ZACH: Are you going to do this?

CASEY: Why not?

ZACH: You better start studying. When is this contest supposed to be, again?

CASEY: January 19th.

ZACH: When's that?

CASEY: Tomorrow night.

ZACH: There's no time.

CASEY: I got the letter a month ago.

ZACH: How come you never told me?

CASEY: You would have forgotten by now.

ZACH: Did your mom say it was okay to do this?

CASEY: She said if I take a friend with me.

ZACH: Can I go?

Casey: You think your mom will let you?

Zach: Yeah.

Casey: You think you'll remember?

[Zach *rolls his eyes.*]

Moontel Six

Constance Congdon

Dramatic

UBERBETH: 13 to 15; a sympathetic girl who is part luminescent jellyfish and has flatulence problems.

ZIPPER: 13 to 15: part lizard and moth.

EMO: 13 to 15; part male goat.

TOYN: 7 to 10; a foundling boy with 100 percent human DNA who is stuck in late babyhood. He has asthma.

Set on the moon, in the future, the play tells the story of a band of teenagers who have been created in labs and contain DNA from other species; hence, they are on the run, pursued by humans who want to sterilize them. In this scene, they've been apprehended by a young human sent into the tunnels to find them and they're trying to explain themselves. At the end of the scene, a young boy emerges—an orphaned human they are protecting. The kids are in a sort of lineup, facing the audience.

UBERBETH: We just want to explain what happened.

ZIPPER: They made us leave.

EMO: They didn't want us.

ZIPPER: At Moonstead Estates, either.

EMO: Particularly there.

ZIPPER: They didn't want us around their kids.

UBERBETH: Because we have these weird genes . . .

EMO: . . . which we didn't ask for.

UBERBETH: But we wouldn't be who we are without them.

EMO: Yeah. There's nothing wrong with us. We're made the way we're made and we're fine with that.

ZIPPER: Uberbeth here is part luminescent jellyfish. [*To* UBERBETH.] Anything glow yet?

UBERBETH: Not so far. But I just began my genitive.

EMO: Yeah, we all have in some way. Zipper's started to pupate.

ZIPPER: I'm waiting for wings and then I get to mate.

UBERBETH: That's really why they didn't want us.

EMO: The whole "mating" thing. As if we'd really even want to date their 100-percent-human Moonstead snobs.

ZIPPER: We have our variations, but we're proud of them. Right?

UBERBETH: Like, I have trouble digesting things with lecithin in it. I'm not sure what lecithin is except it's in anything that has a shelf-life estimate on it.

ZIPPER: So—you don't mind me telling them, do you, Uberbeth?

UBERBETH: Lecithin makes me flatulent.

ZIPPER: And we eat a lot of shelf-life products here.

EMO: We like to think of it as her "special power." And me—I have some genes from some Earth mammal that was supposed to give me really good hair, but, instead it allows me to digest almost anything.

ZIPPER: And I'm part lizard as well as moth. Since lizards eat moths, I have some concerns about my future.

EMO: And we're not 100 percent pure human but, from what I've seen, that's totally fine.

UBERBETH: Only Toyn is totally human. But he has allergies and stuff.

ZIPPER: [*Chastising* UBERBETH.] Uberbeth, you said his name. Now he'll come out.

[TOYN *enters and looks at them—he's holding an inhaler and a "lovey toy"—some shapeless stuffed animal, now unrecognizable. He looks at the audience with suspicion, takes a hit from his inhaler, still looking at them.*]

TOYN: Downloading. Please wait. [*Processes, then suddenly points to individual audience members and identifies them for the kids.*] Analog. Analog. Analog. Analog. All analog. [*Looks closely at one audience member.*] Digital. [*Another audience member, but one that pleases him.*] Vacuum tube unit! Classic.

EMO: Toyn! You're bothering them.

TOYN: Classic.

ZIPPER: They're not androids—except for a few. They're humans, Toyn.

TOYN: [*Speaks to one of the audience members, very deliberately.*] Do not disassemble this unit. Disassembling this unit can cause electrical shock. To you. Danger. Danger. [*He starts to breathe with difficulty—he goes into an attack. The kids run to him and with "Help him" and "Where's the inhaler?" they calm him down.*]

UBERBETH: [*Stroking* TOYN'*s cheek.*] There, there, Toyn.

ZIPPER: So, the deal is, we thought we were Good, but we were perceived as Evil, Bad, and Wrong.

UBERBETH: So we're hoping you'll understand . . .

EMO: . . . the whole story.

Mr. Potcher's Holiday

Bob Silberg

Comic

JAKE: 10 to 13; the other one of Chloe's two political advisors.

CHLOE: 13 to 15; student-body president.

WILL: 10 to 13; one of Chloe's two political advisors.

LORNE: 14 to 15; captain of the football team.

Note: The ages of the characters are flexible. The important thing is that WILL and JAKE should look about the same age as each other, and both should look younger (and ideally be shorter) than CHLOE. LORNE should be large, as befits a football player.

The school's new consultant, Mr. Potcher, has canceled all classes in the arts and all extracurricular activities. The kids have decided that someone should try to change his mind. When CHLOE and the other student leaders wimped out of confronting him, the task fell to Darcy, a girl who does the jobs no one else wants to do in hopes of getting the kids to accept her. CHLOE's political advisors are worried that if Darcy succeeds, she will become so popular that she'll be elected student-body president. Student-body president CHLOE and her two campaign advisors, JAKE and WILL, meet in an otherwise unoccupied classroom.

JAKE: I tell ya, I don't like it!

CHLOE: Simmer down, Jake.

WILL: This could cost us the election, you know!

CHLOE: What are you talking about? They love me!

JAKE: They do, huh? [*He reads from his iPad or phone.*] Statement: Chloe Davenport should be reelected student-body president in the midterm election. Strongly agree: 2 percent. Two percent!!

CHLOE: [*Taken aback.*] Really?

[WILL *reads from his iPad or phone.*]

WILL: Somewhat agree, 38 percent. Somewhat disagree, 47 percent!

JAKE: We're losing them!

CHLOE: But I don't understand. What happened?

WILL: Darcy happened, that's what happened!

JAKE: She's getting big points just for *talking* to Mr. Potcher.

WILL: If she pulls off changing his mind, she could be elected the next president!

CHLOE: But she's not even running.

JAKE: Ever hear of a write-in vote?

WILL: She could be drafted!

[*Football captain* LORNE *opens the classroom door.*]

JAKE: Hey! This is a private meeting!

LORNE: But I forgot my lunch in here.

[WILL *goes to the door and shoves him back out.*]

WILL: Buy it! It's pizza day!

[*He slams the door shut.*]

CHLOE: Are you saying I should've talked to Mr. Potcher?

JAKE: No, no, that would've been too risky if you failed.

WILL: Political suicide!

JAKE: But it leaves you vulnerable if Darcy succeeds!

CHLOE: But it wasn't just me. Lorne and Meryl said they were too busy, too.

WILL: It's different for them.

JAKE: They *need* Darcy to succeed.

WILL: So he can play football.

JAKE: And she can debate.

WILL: Then all they have to do is win a couple of games.

JAKE: A couple of tournaments.

WILL: And no one will remember that they wimped out of talking to Potcher.

JAKE: But for you, it's a question of leadership.

WILL: Leadership!

JAKE: You can't afford to lose that aura right before the midyear election.

WILL: Especially with a fresh, new face in the race.

CHLOE: What can I do?

JAKE and WILL: You've got to confront Darcy!

WILL: She's been playing it cagey.

JAKE: Playing it cutesy.

WILL: No one really knows how her meeting with Potcher went.

JAKE: You've got to change that.

WILL: Find out how she's doing with Potcher.

JAKE: Pin her down!

WILL: Did she change his mind or didn't she?

JAKE: No more waffling!

WILL: And in front of the other kids. As many as possible.

JAKE: The longer she drags this thing out, the worse it is for you!

Pirate Town

Adam Kraar

Seriocomic
THE SISTER: 7
THE LITTLE BOY: 8 to 10

A LITTLE BOY *and his younger* SISTER *walk in the woods. She carries a Barbie doll. He has a ball of string.*

THE SISTER: We're not allowed this far.

THE LITTLE BOY: Then go home.

THE SISTER: Will you take me?

THE LITTLE BOY: Just turn around and go back.

[*Pause.*]

THE SISTER: Where we going?

THE LITTLE BOY: To find the balloon.

THE SISTER: What balloom?

THE LITTLE BOY: The green balloon. Don'tya remember? [*The* SISTER *shakes her head no.*] From Robbie's birthday?

THE SISTER: It flyed away.

THE LITTLE BOY: Yeah; But it's gotta come back down, right? If we go to the thickest part of the woods, we'll find it. Maybe there's lotsa balloons there.

THE SISTER: For real?

THE LITTLE BOY: Yeah.

THE SISTER: How far?

THE LITTLE BOY: Jeez!! Go home. [*Pause.*] What a baby.

THE SISTER: I bet there is no balloom.

THE LITTLE BOY: You saw it!

THE SISTER: It flyed away.

THE LITTLE BOY: Dummy. What goes up must come down. Gravity? [*Pause.*] I let go of it on purpose, 'cause I knew it would come back. [*Pause.*] You come with me, you can have it.

THE SISTER: Really?

THE LITTLE BOY: Yeah. You coming?

THE SISTER: . . . Yeah.

[*They walk. The* SISTER *talks to her doll.*]

THE SISTER: We're gonna find the green balloom. When you rub it, it cries "urrh, urrrh, urrh." There's lotsa other ballooms in there too. Right, Danny?

THE LITTLE BOY: Stop prattling.

THE SISTER: What's "prattling"?

THE LITTLE BOY: [*Hearing something:*] Sssh.

[*He stops. She stops. They listen.*]

THE SISTER: [*Being silly, making a bird noise.*] Coooo.
Coooo.

THE LITTLE BOY: SSSH!

[*They listen for a long time . . .*]

THE SISTER: What if I have to go to the bathroom?

THE LITTLE BOY: D'you hear anything?

THE SISTER: No.

THE LITTLE BOY: You have to go?

THE SISTER: No. But later maybe.

THE LITTLE BOY: Ssh!

THE SISTER: Well. Anyway . . .

THE LITTLE BOY: Anyway what?

THE SISTER: Never mind.

THE LITTLE BOY: You are such a pain!

THE SISTER: You . . . wet your pants.

THE LITTLE BOY: I never!

THE SISTER: You did. That day. From school.

THE LITTLE BOY: You're an idiot.

THE SISTER: Anyway . . .

THE LITTLE BOY: I told you. Some guys sprayed me with a hose. [*Pause.*] I should just leave you here.

THE SISTER: You better not.

THE LITTLE BOY: I could just run off.

THE SISTER: No.

THE LITTLE BOY: You coming? Or not? [*Pause.*] Ah, come on. There's gonna be a lotta ballooms there. You like green, red, or black?

THE SISTER: Green.

THE LITTLE BOY: Then come on.

[*They walk.*]

THE SISTER: Is the string for the balloons?

THE LITTLE BOY: Yep.

THE SISTER: How d'ya know?

THE LITTLE BOY: Logic. Elementary logic. The balloons go up to the end of the atmosphere. By then, they've lost some of their helium. So, gravity pulls 'em back down. Now, when they were up there, they were close to the sun, right? Incredibly hot; blinding light. So, when they come back down, they gravitate to the darkest places. Where it's cool. Like the thickest part of the jungle. Understand?

THE SISTER: Yeah.

THE LITTLE BOY: Now—we may encounter pirates there.

THE SISTER: Pirates?

THE LITTLE BOY: Possibly. We'll proceed with caution. Like garden snakes.

THE SISTER: Snakes?

THE LITTLE BOY: You and I will be like snakes. Quiet.

[*They walk closer together. They are a little apprehensive but also excited and happy to be together on this adventure.*]

THE SISTER: Sorry I said . . .

THE LITTLE BOY: They sprayed me. What could I do?

THE SISTER: Nothing.

THE LITTLE BOY: That's right.

[*They walk in silence.*]

Puppet Play

Evan Guilford-Blake

Comic

SAMANTHA: 10 to 11; KELSEY and BRITTANY's older sister.
KELSEY: 8 to 9; BRITTANY's twin sister.
BRITTANY: 8 to 9; KELSEY's twin sister.

Yesterday, after school. A bedroom, which all three girls share.
KELSEY "loses" her new teddy bear and enlists her sisters' help in
finding it. KELSEY is on the floor, looking for something.
SAMANTHA enters.

SAMANTHA: What are you looking for, Kelsey?

KELSEY: My new teddy bear.

SAMANTHA: Did you look in the closet?

KELSEY: Yes! And under my bed.

SAMANTHA: How about under mine?

KELSEY: Yeah, Samantha. I can't find it!

SAMANTHA: Well, it has to be here somewhere, unless
you—Did you take it downstairs?

KELSEY: I don't think so.

SAMANTHA: Sometimes you do. When you're watching TV.

KELSEY: But I haven't watched TV today.

SAMANTHA: I'll help you look. But maybe we can figure out where you left it.

KELSEY: Okay. Thanks.

SAMANTHA: When you got up this morning, what did you do?

KELSEY: I washed up, got dressed, and I braided Brittany's hair—it got all tangled. She was really mad! Mom had to fix it.

SAMANTHA: Uh-huh. Did you ask her if she saw it?

KELSEY: She's not home yet. She's got her after-school program today.

SAMANTHA: Which one?

KELSEY: Oh, you know, where they use puppets.

SAMANTHA: Oh, that's right. I forgot.

KELSEY: I have to find it. Mom'll kill me! And I won't be able to go to sleep.

SAMANTHA: Was Brittany *really* mad at you? About her hair?

KELSEY: Yeah! She said I did it on purpose!

SAMANTHA: Did you, Kelsey?

KELSEY: Well . . . no. She was just squirming all the time.

SAMANTHA: Maybe she hid it.

KELSEY: Hid it! Oh, Samantha, if she did I'm gonna—hide her stuffed dog!

SAMANTHA: I'm gonna look all the way on top of the closet. Here, hold the chair while I . . .

KELSEY: Can you see it?

SAMANTHA: Not yet, but I can feel something all the way at the back of the shelf.

KELSEY: Reach farther!

SAMANTHA: I'm trying! Hold onto the chair!

[*As she reaches,* BRITTANY *walks in with her backpack.*]

BRITTANY: What are you doing?

SAMANTHA: We're looking for something.

BRITTANY: What?

KELSEY: My teddy bear.

BRITTANY: The new one?

KELSEY: Uh-huh!

BRITTANY: Oh. You look really silly up there, Samantha.

KELSEY: At least she's helping me. *You* hid it!

BRITTANY: Hid it?

KELSEY: Yes!

BRITTANY: You mean this one?

[*She takes a small teddy bear out of her knapsack.*]

SAMANTHA: Where did you get that?!

BRITTANY: Kelsey gave it to me. This morning.

KELSEY: I—. . . Oh, my gosh!

BRITTANY: She said I could take it to use as a puppet in my after-school program because she was sorry she messed up my hair. We did a puppet play of *Goldilocks and the Three Bears*. He was Baby Bear.

SAMANTHA: Did you, Kelsey?

KELSEY: I forgot.

BRITTANY: Here, Kelsey.

KELSEY: Thanks. I'm—sorry, Brittany.

BRITTANY: That's okay. I forget things, too.

SAMANTHA: Like whose turn it is to walk the dog, for example?

BRITTANY: Oh! It's—mine?

SAMANTHA: Uh-huh. And he really, *really* needs to go out.

BRITTANY: Oh, I better hurry. [*She runs out.*]

SAMANTHA: Now you'll be able to get to sleep tonight.

KELSEY: Yeah. But I better do my homework now. I'm going downstairs.

[*She puts the teddy bear on her bed and leaves.*]

SAMANTHA: Okay. See you later. [SAMANTHA *picks up the teddy bear and pretends it's a puppet.*] And you better be good, little girl, or I'll eat all your porridge. And you too! [*She puts the teddy bear on the bed and leaves.*]

Quarry Road

B.J. Burton

Seriocomic

FRANKIE: 15, the pack leader.
PAULIE: 14, the mediator.
CHARLIE: 13: the pensive one, probably wears glasses.

Along Quarry Road—a rural place near a housing development.
FRANKIE runs in carrying a baseball bat. He is sweaty and
anxious. He checks behind him. He waves and gives a signal that
he's running off. He wears torn jeans and a T-shirt, more a
reflection of his economic condition than a fashion statement.

FRANKIE: [*Giving another signal with the bat.*] Ho! Be right
back! [*He exits.* PAULIE *and* CHARLIE *run on, following*
FRANKIE. *They are wearing clothes similar to* FRANKIE's, *but not*
as ragged. CHARLIE *is having a hard time catching his breath.*
PAULIE *notices.*]

PAULIE: Hey, you okay?

CHARLIE: [*Still catching his breath.*] Yeah.

PAULIE: You need your thing-a-ma-what-chis?

CHARLIE: [*Recovering.*] Rescue inhaler? No, I'm okay. I'm not used to running so much.

PAULIE: Nobody can see us now. As soon as the trees start, nobody can see us from here. Flash and I tested it.

[FRANKIE *reenters without the baseball bat.*]

FRANKIE: The bat's hidden, same place as before. Last time, gobs of metal pieces were stuck in it. Took me days to get 'em out. 'Course it's evidence, too, ya know. What's wrong with junior?

CHARLIE: I'm fine.

PAULIE: See? He's fine.

CHARLIE: I'm fine, Frankie.

FRANKIE: Ho, ho! What did I tell you? When we're out in the field, it's "Flash!" Got it?

CHARLIE: "In the field." What are you, FBI?

[PAULIE *laughs.*]

FRANKIE: [*Deadly serious.*] We all got our code names. Paulie, tell him your code name.

PAULIE: [*Rolling his eyes.*] It's Duke.

FRANKIE: See? Are we cool or what? [*To* CHARLIE.] What should we call you?

CHARLIE: My name's Charlie.

FRANKIE: I know, I know. We need to be a little more creative here . . . How 'bout Chickie, short for Chicken?

PAULIE: [*To* FRANKIE.] Careful, man!

FRANKIE: [*To* PAULIE.] Or what? You're as guilty as I am, punk!

CHARLIE: Ah, look, guys, I only came along because Paulie—or rather, Duke—here, said it would be the highlight of the summer, but I fail to see that anything like that has transpired. In fact, I'm quite . . .

FRANKIE: Say what?

PAULIE: Nothin'. [*To* CHARLIE.] Shut it, kid.

FRANKIE: Yeah, let's call him Chickie!

PAULIE: Frankie, really. He's . . .

FRANKIE: Yeah, your kid brother. And you're the one who told him to come with us. He's not old enough.

CHARLIE: Right, I'm not old enough to go mailbox bashing. That's only for smart, older kids like you, Frankie.

FRANKIE: It's a rite of passage! You have no concept of tradition!

CHARLIE: It's lame! You have no concept of lameness!

FRANKIE: You have no concept of courage!

CHARLIE: Courage? You must be kidding! [*He gulps for air.*]

FRANKIE: What's wrong with him?

[CHARLIE *gets out his rescue inhaler and takes a puff.*]

CHARLIE: [*With a cough.*] First of all, Paulie, you should've told me what we were doing. Second, courage is—You think it takes courage to bash someone's mailbox?

FRANKIE: Yeah! You have to time it very carefully, so no one sees ya! Paulie, how long we been doin' this?

PAULIE: Ya know what? I'm done. As of now, I'm done!

FRANKIE: What? You're my best . . .

[PAULIE *moves closer to* CHARLIE.]

PAULIE: We're goin', Frankie.

FRANKIE: [*In shock.*] What?

PAULIE: We. Are. Going.

FRANKIE: But what about our code?

PAULIE: I think I wanna start a new code.

FRANKIE: Ah, Duke, man . . .

PAULIE: It's Paulie. C'mon, Charlie.

[PAULIE *and* CHARLIE *exit.*]

Safe

Penny Jackson

Seriocomic

LIZ: 13
NINA: 13

LIZ and NINA are sitting in LIZ's kitchen. LIZ is skinny; NINA is chubby. They are both eyeing a plate of brownies.

LIZ: Why weren't you in school yesterday?

NINA: I didn't want to go.

LIZ: I don't want to go to school but I still go.

NINA: You know why. Someone left a tub of lard in my locker. And a brochure for Weight Watchers.

LIZ: Who cares what those witches do? Just one more year and we'll be in high school.

NINA: I don't know if I can make it.

LIZ: You were losing weight.

NINA: That diet my doctor made me go on. I hated it. I had to eat only soup that was made out of root vegetables.

LIZ: Ugh! [*She walks over to the plate of brownies.*] My mom said she would pay me twenty bucks for every brownie I ate.

NINA: Wow. How much?

LIZ: I think twenty bucks a brownie.

NINA: Wish someone would pay me every time I ate.

LIZ: But I'm never hungry.

NINA: If you don't start eating again, they'll send you back to the hospital. Please, Liz? Do it for me.

[LIZ *touches the plate, and then withdraws her hand as if it's on fire.*]

LIZ: Okay, Nina. I'm doing this for you. [*She closes her eyes and picks up a brownie. She slowly takes a bite.*]

NINA: Keep going, Liz.

LIZ: I can't do this alone. Please. [NINA *takes a brownie. She consumes it ravenously.*] You're always hungry. I wish I could be like you.

NINA: No, you don't. [*Suddenly, offstage, a baby cries.*] Who's that?

LIZ: That's my sister's baby. That's Sasha?

NINA: Hold on a minute. Where's Sasha?

LIZ: She's in my room.

NINA: What is she doing here? I thought your sister lived in L.A.

LIZ: My sister, who wants to be a movie star, is too busy auditioning—so she left Sasha with us.

[*The baby continues crying.*]

NINA: Aren't you going to do something?

LIZ: What can I do? My mom hired a babysitter who cancelled.

NINA: You got to stop her from crying.

LIZ: But she cries all the time. That's what babies do.

NINA: Liz!

LIZ: All right. [LIZ *stands up and walks out of the room. When she leaves her room,* NINA *begins to eat another brownie.* LIZ *returns with* SASHA *wrapped in a blanket.*] She's finally asleep. Just look at her.

NINA: Oh Liz, she's so beautiful.

LIZ: Haven't you ever held a baby before?

[NINA *shakes her head.* LIZ *tenderly places the baby in* NINA's *arms.*]

NINA: She's so light. Just like a feather.

LIZ: Close your eyes.

NINA: What?

LIZ: Close your eyes and hold Sasha tight.

[NINA *clutches the baby to her chest.*]

NINA: I can feel her heartbeat!

LIZ: Breathe in and breathe out.

NINA: Yes . . .

LIZ: Are you floating?

NINA: I feel so light . . .

LIZ: This is what it's like when you love someone.

[*For a few seconds,* NINA *looks as if she's in rapture. She turns to* LIZ.]

NINA: Thank you.

Seph

Monica Flory

Dramatic

NAV: 14, a boy
SEPH: 13, a girl

SEPH has been stolen by HADES to become Queen of the Underworld. She is bewildered. NAV enters and whispers to her.

NAV: Are you okay?

SEPH: What?

NAV: He's a heavy sleeper.

SEPH: How do you know?

NAV: I live here. Are you okay?

SEPH: I think so.

NAV: Good. You're not dead, are you?

SEPH: I don't think so. You?

NAV: Dead.

SEPH: You're so young.

NAV: It was an accident. It's not so bad.

SEPH: Oh. Do you know how I got here?

NAV: Stolen, I guess. From the Aboveworld.

SEPH: Yes.

NAV: There's no sun here.

SEPH: I'll miss it.

NAV: But there are other things. You'll see.

SEPH: You have something on your arm.

[She reaches to brush it off.]

NAV: Don't!

[HADES stirs. NAV hides until HADES sleeps again.]

SEPH: I'm sorry.

NAV: You can't touch here. You can't laugh. It's the only way you'll ever leave.

SEPH: What's on your arm?

NAV: Moss. I can scrape it off again, but it will be back by morning.

SEPH: Oh.

NAV: I'm starting to get it everywhere. You have to keep yourself from turning back into earth, you know?

SEPH: I've never heard of that.

NAV: You'll hear a lot of things if you stick around long enough.

SEPH: How do I get out of here?

NAV: Don't eat anything, no matter how hungry you get. Don't cry, even if you think you can't help it. Observers are everywhere, and if they catch you doing anything human, you're stuck here forever.

SEPH: I'll get hungry.

NAV: Everyone does. You get pretty desperate. I'd gladly take a kick to the face if I could cry about it afterwards.

SEPH: You're funny.

NAV: Sometimes I just pretend I'm a tree. A tree can feel things, in the roots, in the centermost circle of their trunk. In the core. But there are so many circles and branches and leaves that to us it just looks like a tree. You can't even tell it's feeling something, you know?

SEPH: Yeah. I'm a tree.

NAV: You have to try to remember as much as you can. Keep it tucked away, in your core—but keep it.

SEPH: Remember.

NAV: Can you think of anything from home right now?

SEPH: My birthday. I turned thirteen. And I was picking a daffodil for my mother. Red.

NAV: When you lie in bed at night, try to remember as much as you can before you fall asleep. It's the only way. And then we can talk about it the next day. I'll help you.

SEPH: What do you remember?

NAV: One thing. I was little. My mom had her branches wrapped around me. Her arms. And she was singing.

SEPH: What song?

NAV: I can't remember. [*Pause.*] Trees need sleep here. You should try to get some.

SEPH: Next to him?

NAV: [*Nodding.*] If you get scared, touch the ground.

SEPH: I'm a tree.

NAV: Same roots. Sweet dreams.

Smoldering Fires

Kermit Frazier

Dramatic

COREY: 12, African American
DASHAUN: 12, African American

COREY *and* DASHAUN *are best friends living in a sometimes violent, drug-infested urban neighborhood. This scene takes place toward the beginning of act 1. The boys have just come from school and have raced each other to their favorite place in a park where they can hang out some before heading home.* DASHAUN *had been in the principal's office at their middle school, where he was reprimanded for nearly getting into a fight with another boy.* COREY *gave a book report in class on* Freedom's Children *(a nonfiction book written by Ellen Levine and published by Putnam in 1993) about activist young people during the civil rights movement. The boys run in and set down their backpacks.*

COREY: [*Breathlessly.*] Caught you and beat you. [*They take off their backpacks while catching their breath.*] I'm always gonna be faster than you, D.

DASHAUN: Maybe. But you ain't never gonna be as big. Or as fly.

COREY: And that's why you got it on with Harold?

DASHAUN: No. Wasn't about all that. It was nothing.

COREY: Nothing? It was enough to make you miss my book report.

DASHAUN: Oh, yeah. How was it? Bet it was tight.

COREY: Tight as can be.

[*They pound fists.*]

DASHAUN: You got an A?

COREY: A-plus.

DASHAUN: Man, see. There you go again. That's why I be getting C's and D's in English.

COREY: What do you mean?

DASHAUN: Okay. It's my theory of balance, see. I figure that the whole class has got to be balanced out. And you keep on stretching the class way, way up there. So to even it out, somebody's got to be stretching it way, way down here.

COREY: And that somebody's got to be you?

DASHAUN: Hey, what are friends for?

COREY: You're crazy.

DASHAUN: I know.

[*They laugh.*]

COREY: But hey, check it out. [*He takes his paperback copy of* Freedom's Children *from his backpack.*]

DASHAUN: [*Reading the book cover.*] *Freedom's Children* . . . Must not be about us.

COREY: No, but it *is* about black kids. How they marched and demonstrated and fought for integration. You know, the civil rights movement.

DASHAUN: Oh, yeah, all that stuff way back when.

COREY: Not so way back. Wanna read it?

DASHAUN: Man, you know reading gives me a headache.

COREY: This won't.

DASHAUN: I don't know, Corey. Shoot, if they fought so hard for integration, how come we don't have any around here?

COREY: Huh?

DASHAUN: Well, integration is like mixing, right? Folks all mixed up together?

COREY: I guess. Sorta.

DASHAUN: Well, do you see any white people living around here?

COREY: Okay, but that's not the only thing about integration. I mean, we can go anywhere we want to now. Movie theaters, stores, amusement parks, beaches. Back then, black people couldn't even use the same drinking fountains as white people.

DaShaun: I know all that. I know we can "go" places. But people ain't always happy to be seeing us when we *do* go places. [*Looking toward downtown.*] It's almost like they wanna be stopping us sometimes. White people's eyes all up on us like we're gonna be ripping them off.

Corey: Not all of them. Just because some white people don't like us doesn't mean they all don't.

DaShaun: And just 'cause they like *you* don't mean they like *me*.

Corey: Well, I know one or two *black* people who don't like you either.

DaShaun: Fo' sho'.

Corey: Why'd you fight him *this* time?

DaShaun: [*Reluctant to say.*] I don't know. . . . I just wish I had me some better clothes.

Corey: You look all right.

DaShaun: [*Defensive despite himself.*] I know I look all right.

Corey: He talked about your clothes? [DaShaun *says nothing.*] Man, don't you even wanna graduate from middle school?

DaShaun: Yeah, like *tomorrow*, yo. [*He looks up at the sky.*] Man, I sure wish I had me a pilot's license. And my own personal jet. I'd be able to go anywhere at any time.

Corey: You'd be a great pilot.

DaShaun: Yeah, I know. Zooming across the sky. [*Looking around.*] And maybe I'd even drop a bomb or two on certain rundown things around here.

Corey: It'd be better if we could fix stuff up. This ole park, some of the houses. And kick out all the drug dealers.

DaShaun: Well, you can forget that. They ain't going nowhere ever.

Corey: They will if my Moms and Pops have anything to say about it.

DaShaun: Yeah, they're all right, your Moms and Pops.

Corey: Your grandma's not so bad either.

DaShaun: Except when she gets on me. Also, she's getting kind of old all of a sudden. Gonna be fifty soon.

Corey: Fifty?

DaShaun: Uh-huh. And I got about zero dollars to buy her a present with.

Corey: Wow, fifty!

[DaShaun *begins beating out a rap rhythm.*]

DaShaun: To make fifty put the five and zero together
It'll make you feel cool no matter the weather

Or not you're too hot or going down slow
To the sto' on the corner
Whenever you wanna
'Cause you're still my fine Grams
Who cooks me chicken and ham
And all the other things I like
To keep me hopping and psyched
And . . .
[*Faltering.*]
And . . . got no more rhymes my head
'Cause . . .

COREY: [*Rapping.*] Your feet's full of lead.

DASHAUN: Yo, what?

COREY: Just trying to help.

DASHAUN: Thanks.

COREY: I know. You could finish that rap and make *that* your grandma's birthday present. That'd be free.

DASHAUN: Naw, it's got to be a thing. A big, expensive thing!

COREY: But you don't have any money.

DASHAUN: I'll get me some somehow.

COREY: You could bag some groceries.

DASHAUN: Chump change.

COREY: Not if you keep saving it.

DaShaun: Shoot, I'd be fifty myself by the time I'd saved enough. [*Pause.*] I just want stuff, Corey. You know?

Corey: I know. Me, too.

DaShaun: A big ole house.

Corey: A big backyard.

DaShaun: A big-screen TV.

Corey: A little red sports car.

DaShaun: A girl I can talk to. [DaShaun *and* Corey *suddenly look at each other, both a little embarrassed. They just as quickly look away.*] Well, you know . . .

Corey: Oh, man, I'm gonna be late.

DaShaun: [*Jumping up.*] Yeah, let's bounce.

Corey: See you tomorrow, D.

DaShaun: Yeah, all up in school.

Corey: [*Taking out the book.*] Wait, the book.

[DaShaun *looks at the book, then takes it reluctantly.*]

DaShaun: Thanks.

[*The boys pound fists.*]

Smoldering Fires

Kermit Frazier

Dramatic

COREY: 12, African American
DASHAUN: 12, African American

COREY *and* DASHAUN *are 12-year-old African American boys. They are best friends living in a sometimes violent, drug-infested, urban neighborhood. This scene takes place toward the end of act 1.* DASHAUN *has been at home because he has been suspended for fighting in the schoolyard (actually defending* COREY*), when he suddenly decides in frustration that he will accept drug dealer Willis's offer to be a "slinger" for him. But when he gets to Willis's,* DASHAUN *overhears the dealer plotting with an addict to get revenge on* COREY*'s parents for their neighborhood "stop the drugs" campaign. With that,* DASHAUN *rushes away. In this scene,* COREY *has met* DASHAUN *at their hangout spot in the park.*

COREY: But that doesn't mean he's going to do anything, D.

DASHAUN: I'm just saying what I heard.

COREY: Well, my mom's got a lot of signatures on the petition already. So she's got a lot of people behind her. Besides, my dad can take care of any ole nodded-out junkie.

DASHAUN: Not if he takes you by surprise.

COREY: By doing what?

DASHAUN: I don't know. I didn't go up and ask him.

COREY: What were you doing hanging around Willis anyway?

DASHAUN: I wasn't hanging.

COREY: What then? [DASHAUN *says nothing. Something suddenly dawns on* COREY.] Oh, man.

DASHAUN: Look, my grandma's birthday is soon, awright?

COREY: So you're slinging for Willis now?

DASHAUN: No! . . . I mean . . . he offered me something yesterday and I was about ready to play. But then I heard what he said to Bogus and . . . I changed my mind.

COREY: So you're not slinging?

DASHAUN: What did I just say, Corey? Man . . .

COREY: Okay, okay. . . . So now you can sign my mom's petition. And help me with the park thing. That's how *we're* gonna play it.

DASHAUN: For free?

COREY: It's what we've gotta do, D. Or at least try. [DASHAUN *says nothing.*] I really feel bad about you getting suspended. And all because of me.

DASHAUN: It wasn't just because of you.

COREY: I don't mind being called "shrimpie," you know. Or "shake 'n' bake."

DASHAUN: I would.

COREY: I know that. [*With a laugh.*] You wouldn't have lasted one second during the civil rights thing. You would have been throwing punches and jumping people if they even *looked* at you funny.

DASHAUN: Yeah, well, that's the way it is, Corey, awright?

COREY: But it doesn't have to be that way. You know, in *Freedom's Children* . . .

DASHAUN: Lay off about that book, Corey, awright?

COREY: Okay. Sorry. [*Awkward pause.*] What'd your grandma say?

DASHAUN: She grounded me for the three days of my suspension and another week after that.

COREY: Then how can you be here?

DASHAUN: I had to tell you, man.

COREY: Yeah, but even before now you were. . .

DASHAUN: Look, I'm gonna be back before she gets home. Stop worrying about me.

COREY: Hey, you worry about me. [*They look away from each other, slightly embarrassed. Then:*] Well, at least you've got more time to work on that free birthday present. Your "Fifty Rap."

DASHAUN: Yeah, right.

COREY: How's it coming?

DASHAUN: It's not.

COREY: Hey, I know. We could do a rap together.

DASHAUN: About being fifty?

COREY: No, no, about anything. For practice. To get your words flowing. We could do the . . . the "Petition Rap."

DASHAUN: How about the "Stomp Harold Rap?"

COREY: Come on, man.

DASHAUN: I'm just shouting out.

COREY: [*Getting excited.*] Hey, hey. Maybe we could "rap" all the drug dealers up and send them FedEx to the North Pole.

DASHAUN: Humm. . . . Wait a minute. [*He begins to bang out a beat.*]
Now it wouldn't be too cold
In fact, it'd be big and bold
If we could rap up some dudes
And send them straight to the Pole.

COREY: [*Jumping in.*]
Uh . . . uh, polar bears to the right
Snowdrifts to the left
And a temperature so low
They're gonna always see their breath.

[*The boys take bold stances and slap fives, then stop and pull back.*]

Needs a lotta work, right?

DASHAUN: A *whole* lotta work. [*They laugh.*] But it could be goin' on. We could call ourselves the CD Players.

COREY: I like that. Especially with the "C" coming first.

DASHAUN: Uh-huh.

COREY: Well, I *am* the oldest. By one whole month.

DASHAUN: True 'dat, "Shrimpie."

COREY: [*Feigning indignation.*] Don't call me that.

DASHAUN: Why? What you gonna do? Protest? Rap me over the head?

COREY: Your grandma's gonna be rapping you if you don't get home soon.

DASHAUN: Naw, she don't do no corporal punishment.

COREY: Not yet, you mean.

DASHAUN: So let's kick it then. [*He takes off running.*]

COREY: Hey, no fair! [*He takes off after him.*]

Sweet Teeth

Fran Handman

Comic

MARTA: 10 to 15
JOSÉ: 10 to 15
TAYISHA: 10 to 15
CARMEN: 10 to 15

Note: Characters could alternatively be MARTA, JOSÉ, PEDRO, and CARMEN.

Four kids are sitting on a stoop in front of a house.

MARTA: I know how dinosaurs became extinct.

JOSÉ: Marta, are you going to tell us one of your silly stories again?

TAYISHA: Don't bother. We just want to hang out.

MARTA: You guys never want to learn anything. You really want to grow up ignorant?

CARMEN: So, you're going to educate us, right?

JOSÉ: Okay, okay. You're going to tell us anyway, so go ahead. How did the dinosaurs become extinct?

MARTA: You know that dinosaurs were pretty big, right?

TAYISHA: Right, so far.

MARTA: Which made them pretty clumsy.

JOSÉ: Uh-huh.

MARTA: Well, the small, fleet-footed dinosaurs used to throw parties.

TAYISHA: Dinosaurs threw parties? Come on, Marta.

MARTA: Why not? They had birthdays just like anyone else.

JOSÉ: And did they sing "Happy Birthday" to each other?

MARTA: Okay, guys. You don't want to hear this—never mind.

CARMEN: No, go on. We're all ears.

MARTA: Okay, so all the dinosaurs would be invited. But, because the really big dinosaurs were so clumsy, they never got to the parties on time and they always missed the treats. There they'd be, finally at the party, huffing and puffing and no ice cream and no cake.

TAYISHA: Ice cream! Cake! Whoa!

MARTA: Come on. You think you're so smart. You've heard of ice floes. Well, those dinosaurs were pretty inventive. They wanted ice cream. They figured it out. They got ice from the ice floes and they stomped on it until it was in little chips and then they added shrimp. And there it was. Shrimp ice cream.

CARMEN: What? This story is even crazier than usual. I suppose they had lobster pie, too.

MARTA: They didn't have lobster then. But sometimes they added a green onion and made shrimp-onion ice cream. It gave it a special tang.

JOSÉ: And maybe a dash of paprika.

TAYISHA: And what did they put in the cake—tomatoes?

MARTA: You're getting too wise, Tayisha. I'll tell you about the cake. Where they lived, those dinosaurs, it was very, very hot and the ground got baked and caked.

ALL: Oh, no!!!

MARTA: They would cut out a round chunk of the caked earth, add a few insects and use melted shrimp ice cream for icing. They loved it. It was good for their digestion and it was a cure for wheezing.

CARMEN: So when is the extinct part of the story? So far all we got is some dinosaur recipes.

MARTA: Well, if you weren't so busy criticizing, you would remember that those big, clumsy dinosaurs never got any of that cake and ice cream. You think they just smiled and said, "No problem, that's all right. We came from far away under a hot sun and nobody left nothing for us. Thank you so much." You think they did that?

JOSÉ: So what did they do?

Marta: Well, first they kicked up a ruckus and, of course, they were never invited to any of the fleet-footed dinosaurs' parties again.

Carmen: That's it. This is a story about party rejects and that's how they became extinct, because they didn't have shrimp-onion ice cream?

Marta: Whoa, Carmen. You are really stupid. Would I tell you a dumb story like that?

José: Yes.

Marta: I'll ignore that. Anyway, those dinosaurs might be clumsy but they were smart. They would make their own ice cream—and not with shrimp but with sugar.

Carmen: Where would they get sugar?

Marta: You ever heard of sweet-water lakes?

Ayisha: There isn't any sugar in sweet-water lakes.

Marta: Were you there? Where do you think they got the name of "sweet-water." Well, just by accident, one of the big dinosaurs was swimming in one of those lakes and said, "Wow, this is really sweet water. It would taste better in ice cream than shrimp does. We'll show them. We'll have our own parties." And then they all stood around the lake and breathed on the water until it evaporated, and then they collected the sugar that was left.

José: So, now, we have another dinosaur recipe and the dinosaurs are still not extinct. I'm ready to go get some ice cream. [*To all.*] How about you guys?

MARTA: I can't believe you. You've only heard the lead-up and now you're going to miss the big ending?

JOSÉ: One more minute, and then I'm gone.

MARTA: Okay, I'll tell you. When word got around that sweet ice cream had been invented, nobody went to the fleet-footed dinosaurs' parties anymore. They all came for the sweet ice cream—and they not only ate it at parties, but every day.

AYISHA: We're leaving, Marta. So far, no extinct dinosaurs.

MARTA: What happens when you eat sugar day after day?

CARMEN: You get fat.

MARTA: You get cavities. You've never seen anything until you've seen a bunch of dinosaurs running around with toothaches.

JOSÉ: Are you trying to tell us that every last dinosaur died of a toothache?

MARTA: You're joking. Who would believe that? What happened was that they all lost their teeth and then they couldn't eat. It was pretty hard to gum down a mastodon. So they all died. And that's how they became extinct.

T.M.S.
(Total Male Syndrome)

Claudia I. Hass

Comic

LIZA: 12 to 13; a perfectionist.
ROB: 12 to 13; a clueless young teen.
HANNAH: 12 to 13; a down-to-earth pragmatic.
JESSIE: 12 to 13; a teen who is tired of doing all the work.

Wrappings and ribbons are scattered in LIZA's living room, as the kids attempt to wrap toys for a holiday service project from school. ROB is playing video games. LIZA holds up a present not beautifully wrapped. There may be other scattered presents—also not beautifully wrapped—as well as some bags of toys.

LIZA: I can't do this! Why is nothing looking pretty? I think we should have a theme.

ROB: What are you talking about?

LIZA: You know, like everything is sparkly gold with matching ribbons—or red and green. Something that ties them all together.

HANNAH: Are you thinking that the kids care more about the wrapping than the toy? [HANNAH *also holds up a not-perfectly-wrapped present.*]

LIZA: I do!

JESSIE: Well, it would be nice to have them beautiful. But too expensive. We'd have to buy all new paper and bows. Let's just use the donated stuff? What do you think, Rob?

ROB: [*Intent on the game.*] Come on! Go! GO! YES! [*Back to* LIZA *and* HANNAH.] What?

LIZA: Don't you think it would look nicer for the kids if all the wrapping and bows and ribbons matched?

ROB: Yeah. Sure. Whatever.

HANNAH: Liza! The kids are just going to tear them apart in one minute. It doesn't make sense to buy all new wrapping. What do you think, Rob?

ROB: That works. [*Back to video games.*] NO!

JESSIE: He's not listening.

HANNAH: I know.

ROB: What?

HANNAH: T.M.S.

LIZA: Totally.

ROB: What?

JESSIE: You could help, you know. You're getting credit for this also.

ROB: What?

LIZA: If you don't do some work, we'll throw you off the project.

ROB: What are you talking about?

HANNAH: Your service hours. You're not doing anything! No honor roll for you!

LIZA: He'll use the T.M.S. defense.

JESSIE: Definitely.

ROB: T.M.S.?

HANNAH: Total Male Syndrome. You have it. My dad has it. Every boy in school has it.

ROB: What?

LIZA: [*Talking to him like he is three years old.*] It's an inability to hear what females are saying. You have selective hearing. All guys do. It's in your genes.

ROB: What?

HANNAH: Go back to your video games.

ROB: No, really. I want to know what you are saying.

JESSIE: Wow! A cohesive sentence. We got his attention. Now—get him to do some work.

HANNAH: [*Handing him a toy.*] Here you go, Rob. Get wrapping.

ROB: What? You want me to sing? I can't rap. I can't keep all those words in my head.

HANNAH: W-R-A-P, Rob! Help us. We did the shopping. We picked the names. We planned everything. What are you—along for the ride?

ROB: I'll go. Where're we going?

LIZ: We were speaking metaphorically, Rob!

ROB: Metaphors? More English class? I thought we were doing a service project.

JESSIE: Wow. His T.M.S. is very advanced.

ROB: What do you want me to do? Just tell me and I'll do it.

LIZA: Am I talking? Does he hear me? I hear me. You hear me. ROB, DO YOU HEAR ME?

ROB: You don't have to yell.

LIZA: Grrrr! This is frustrating me. I need some cookies.

ROB: Cookies? Did I hear "cookies"?

LIZA: Your selective hearing works well, Rob. I'm getting some cookies. Mom baked Christmas cookies yesterday. Maybe a sugar rush will help.

JESSIE: How about some music?

LIZA: Sounds good. I need all the inspiration I can get!

ROB: What do you want me to do?

LIZA and HANNAH and JESSIE: Wrap some presents!

[LIZA *runs into the kitchen while* HANNAH *puts on some music.* ROB *takes some wrapping supplies and toys and goes off to a corner—possibly near his video games.* JESSIE *works.*]

HANNAH: What do you want to hear?

JESSIE: 'Tis the season stuff.

[LIZA *comes back with a plate of cookies.*]

LIZA: Where's Rob?

HANNAH: Over in the corner. Probably figuring out some new strategy for the video game.

LIZA: Should we call him over to help? When you have T.M.S. sometimes you need things spelled out for you. Like . . . [*Loudly.*] . . . if you want service hours, you need to put in the time!

ROB: [*Loudly.*] You already said that. Why are you being so repetitive?

JESSIE: Look at him over there—clueless. Clueless that we are doing all the work.

LIZA: Maybe if we tell him about the cookies.

ROB: Sugar cookies or butter?

HANNAH: There's hope for him yet! Rob! For every present you wrap, you get a cookie!

LIZA: Maybe we should offer him two. His Total Male Syndrome is way advanced. Wrapping one present could be pretty hard for him. I feel sorry for him.

HANNAH: Okay—he gets two cookies for every present.

LIZA: ROB! Two cookies for every present you wrap. Deal?

ROB: Deal. [*He comes over with three absolutely perfectly beautifully wrapped presents, complete with bows.*] That's six cookies you owe me. So far.

LIZA: How . . . ?

HANNAH: Why didn't you tell us you could wrap presents?

ROB: You didn't ask.

JESSIE: How . . . how did you learn to do that?

ROB: It's all those video games. Develops hand-eye coordination. Very good for making perfect corners. It's really helpful when you need to make the bows. [*Eyeing the cookie plate.*]

I hope you have a lot more cookies. That Total Male Syndrome stuff—I think you're on to something. Yep, I need all the help I can get.

[*He pops a cookie in his mouth as the lights fade to black.*]

Verona

Don Nigro

Dramatic

VONNIE: 15, a girl
PITT: 14, a boy

The setting is the stage of the Odessa Theatre, in the small east Ohio town of Armitage, before rehearsal on a late autumn afternoon in 1897. VONNIE *is memorizing her lines. She has a little hardback copy of* Romeo and Juliet. *She reads her lines very simply and well. She's quite good. She's 15 and very beautiful.* PITT *watches her. He's 14, scrawny, and not all that clean. They are both in rehearsal for a community production of Shakespeare's* Romeo and Juliet, *in which* VONNIE *plays Juliet and* PITT *has a small role as a comic servant. The production is being directed by James Rose, their young English teacher at the high school.* VONNIE *is the daughter of a storekeeper; she is the smartest girl in her class. She is a girl with a clear eye and an independent soul.* PITT *is the possibly illegitimate son of a junkyard owner, and has grown up next to the town dump. He is very much aware of his family's low status in the community. The lines* VONNIE *is working on in her first speech are Juliet's lines, spoken when she is waiting impatiently for Romeo.*

VONNIE: Come, night; come Romeo; come, thou day in night;
for thou wilt lie upon the wings of night
whiter than new snow on a raven's back.
Come, gentle night. Come, loving, black-browed night,
Give me my Romeo; and when he shall die,
Take him and cut him out in little stars,
And he will make the face of Heaven so fine
That all the world will be in love with night,
And pay no . . . and pay no worship . . .

[*Looking up*, VONNIE *sees* PITT *there.*]

VONNIE: What are you looking at?

PITT: I saw you.

VONNIE: You saw what?

PITT: I saw you.

VONNIE: I don't know what you mean.

PITT: I saw what he did.

VONNIE: What who did?

PITT: What he did. I saw it.

VONNIE: What are you talking about?

PITT: I know what you're doing.

VONNIE: I'm trying to learn my lines. That's what I'm doing. If you'd just go away.

PITT: You think people don't see you? Do you think people don't know?

VONNIE: I don't know what people don't know. I don't know what you're talking about.

PITT: You think you're better.

VONNIE: Better than what?

PITT: Just because your father has a store. And we live at the junkyard by the dump.

VONNIE: I don't care where you live.

PITT: I been watching you.

VONNIE: Well, stop it.

PITT: I been watching.

VONNIE: Have you been peeking in our windows at night? Because my father's got a shotgun and he knows how to use it.

PITT: I know what you are.

VONNIE: You know what I am?

PITT: I know.

VONNIE: Well, if you know what I am, I wish you'd tell me. Because I'd like to know what I am. I been trying to figure that out for a long time now. But the only time I feel real is when I'm being somebody else.

PITT: Somebody should tell his wife.

VONNIE: Tell whose wife?

PITT: What you're doing.

VONNIE: I'm playing Juliet at the Odessa Theatre. That's what I'm doing. I don't know what you're doing.

PITT: You're playing something all right.

VONNIE: Will you please leave me alone? Will you just go away and leave me alone?

PITT: You think because we live at the junkyard by the dump, we're stupid. But I'm not stupid. I got eyes and ears and a brain just like you, and I can see what's going on. I know what you are. I know what you do. After rehearsal.

VONNIE: I don't do anything after rehearsal. After rehearsal, I go home.

PITT: Don't treat me like I'm stupid. He touches you. I've seen him touch you. He was kissing you. I saw you.

VONNIE: I don't know what you think you saw, but it wasn't what you think. He was helping me with the scenes. He was showing me how to do the scenes.

PITT: He was showing you more than that. And you were showing him.

VONNIE: You're crazy. You are completely out of your filthy, filthy mind.

PITT: [Starting to go.] I'm going to tell his wife.

VONNIE: Pitt. Don't do that. Pitt. [*She runs after him and gets between him and the door.*] Don't do that.

PITT: Why shouldn't I?

VONNIE: Because you're wrong.

PITT: I'm not wrong. You know I'm not wrong.

VONNIE: Because it would hurt her.

PITT: I don't care about that. I come from the junkyard by the dump and you think I care if some schoolteacher's wife gets hurt because of what her rotten husband's doing with a teenage girl backstage after rehearsal?

VONNIE: What do you want?

PITT: What do I want?

VONNIE: Just tell me what you want.

PITT: If I tell your father, he'll take that shotgun and kill him.

VONNIE: Pitt, just tell me. Tell me what you want.

PITT: Look at me.

VONNIE: I am looking at you.

PITT: You're looking at me, but you're not seeing me. You never see me. It's like I'm invisible. You treat me like the furniture. Or some kind of stray dog. Except you'd pet the stray dog. But I look at you. I see how you push your hair back from your face. I see you when you take your shoes off and put your feet in the creek. I see your hands. The patterns your hands make in the air when you talk. I see what you do with your tongue when you lick your lips. I see everything. But you don't see me. Nobody sees me. [*Pause.*]

VONNIE: I'm sorry.

PITT: I'll bet you are.

VONNIE: I'm sorry I don't look at you.

PITT: You're sorry I caught you.

VONNIE: What do you want from me, Pitt? Because, all right, I wasn't looking at you before, but I'm looking at you now. Just tell me what you want and maybe I can . . . [*Pause.*]

PITT: What I want. [*Pause.*] What I want, you can't give me.

VONNIE: Then I don't know what to do. I don't know what that means, and I don't know what to do.

PITT: Do you think he's going to leave his wife for some teenage girl? Is that what you think?

VONNIE: No.

PITT: Is that what you want?

VONNIE: No.

PITT: Then what do you want?

VONNIE: I don't know. I don't know what I want.

PITT: Then what are you doing?

VONNIE: I don't know what I'm doing.

PITT: I could kill him for you.

VONNIE: What?

PITT: I could kill him for you. Easy. I kill things all the time. I know how to kill things. That's something I know how to do.

VONNIE: I don't want anybody to kill anybody.

PITT: I could make it look like an accident. Nobody would ever know it had anything to do with you.

VONNIE: Pitt. You listen to me. Don't you hurt him. I mean it. Don't you ever, ever hurt him.

PITT: You love him.

VONNIE: I don't want him hurt.

PITT: He doesn't love you.

VONNIE: I don't want to talk about this.

PITT: How could you let him touch you?

VONNIE: I don't know.

PITT: Did you want him to touch you?

VONNIE: That's none of your business.

PITT: Because either you didn't want him to touch you, which means he deserves to be killed, or you did want him to touch you, which means you're a whore. So which is it, Vonnie?

VONNIE: Don't call me a whore. I'm not a whore.

PITT: Then what are you?

VONNIE: I'm sorry you're unhappy. I am. I know what it feels like, to have nobody to talk to. Nobody to be with. I know how lonely it is.

PITT: You don't know anything about it.

VONNIE: I do. [*She reaches out to touch his face.*]

PITT: [*Pulling away from her.*] You think you can touch me and that'll make it all right? Is that what you think? Because, let me tell you. That doesn't make anything all right. Nothing ever makes anything all right. And don't you be sorry for me. Don't you be sorry. Don't you ever be sorry.

[PITT *goes.* VONNIE *stands there looking after him.*]

Vikings/Mermaids

Reina Hardy

Dramatic

JARED: 15, a boy
SIGMA: 15, a girl

*In the middle of the lake at Camp Teen Adventure, a teenage
loner sketches a fantasy girl, and connects with a real one.* JARED
paddles to the middle of the lake.

Note: Kayaks are easily and rather wonderfully
represented by office chairs straddled backwards.

JARED: "There is no companion so companionable as
solitude." —Thoreau. Far from the chattering hordes
playing beach volleyball, the lake is an undisturbed
kingdom, and the solitary man is its king. Around him,
water. Beyond that, the quiet trees. Far from the chattering
hordes, the beach volleyball, and Daniel Polenberg, the
kayak supervisor. [*Gives the thumbs-up sign. Shouts:*] I'M
OKAY, DANNY—a man can get down to the business of
his soul. Drawing his own porn, and then using it. [JARED
extracts a notebook and pencil and begins to draw.] Okay . . . a
mermaid? Mermaids. Floating just below the surface, they
beckon the solitary traveller—their fingers like whispers,

their eyes like pleas, their breasts like engraved invitations. Their voices are the cries of birds, their gentle laughter is water—

SIGMA: SPIRIT WORLD VIKINGS AHOY! [*She paddles up to* JARED. JARED *hides his notebook.*] Greetings to my fellow Spirit World Viking. Ahoy, brother. Watcha doing out here by yourself?

JARED: Nothing. Kayak practice. God.

SIGMA: Do you know, if we really were Vikings, and dead, we could be on fire right now?

JARED: Yes, I did know that, actually.

SIGMA: How's kayak practice going? Can you do a roll yet?

JARED: I . . .

SIGMA: I can. Check it out. [*She rolls, comes up, and shakes her hair.*] You should try it. It looks like danger, but it's awesome to get all wet.

JARED: I heard this lake has a rating of 3.4 billion microbes per liter. Including chlamydia.

SIGMA: You're no fun, you know that?

JARED: I've been told. Maybe you'd like to go away now. [*She splashes him with her paddle.*] Ow, what the hell?

SIGMA: Here's chlamydia in your eye. Jared, I'll be honest. I saw this little lonely speck in the middle of the water, and I knew right away who it was. We all know you haven't been quote-unquote "fitting in," or quote-unquote "enthusiastically participating in team activities." All the other Spirit World Vikings are playing kayak polo down in South Lake.

JARED: And you're not with them—why?

SIGMA: Kayak polo sucks. I have better things to do. Like rescue my brother Viking—

JARED: From?

SIGMA: Watcha drawing?

JARED: I wasn't—I'm not—

[SIGMA *grabs for his notebook. They struggle.*]

JARED: Hey this is dangerous, this is not cool— DANNY—NOT OK—NOT OK—you are breaking the prime law of kayak safety, cease and desist—WATCH YOUR PADDLE—

[SIGMA *wins and paddles away with the notebook.*]

JARED: Give me back my notebook, you braying lunatic!

SIGMA: Come and get it. Or just float there, abiding by the prime law.

JARED: Danny!

SIGMA: Holy cats. Ariel without her shells. Gee, she's growing up.

JARED: No, okay, look no. That's not the little mermaid. It doesn't look like Disney. Can't you recognize Satoshi Kon–influenced anime style when you see it?

SIGMA: I recognize fish girls with nipples.

JARED: Can you give me back my property now?

SIGMA: You shouldn't be embarrassed. At least it's good cartoon porn. You could sell it in your cabin.

JARED: It's not porn—it's art. And it's private.

SIGMA: Really? I thought only girls needed privacy for that sort of thing. I thought you all just lined up in your cabins and did it into a trough, like a row of spigots. She's very pretty.

JARED: Thank you. [*Pause.*] So. Um. So. [*Pause.*] I'm sorry about your dad.

SIGMA: Shut up, Jared.

JARED: I . . . what? I'm sorry, you just . . . stopped talking, so I thought . . .

SIGMA: Jared, your cold-hearted asshole-dom is the only reason I like you. Don't you dare start turning into the kind of person who gives a shit.

JARED: I don't. Give a shit.

SIGMA: I'm sure you'd like walking around in a princess tragedy crown, doing your slam poetry all the time, but that's not me. Does it ever occur to any of you that I don't want to think about it all the time? Can there be like, one person at this stupid camp who doesn't have to make every conversation a group hug?

JARED: I don't do slam poetry.

SIGMA: Then why do you always wear that hat? [*Pause.*]. This is a weird day. The lake is so flat. So undisturbed.

JARED: Dead wind.

SIGMA: Make a ripple.

[JARED *uses his paddle to disturb the lake.*]

JARED: Look—it's going to go all the way back to the beach. [*He gives the thumbs-up sign.*] All clear, Danny. The light is kind of doing something to your face. Like half of it is sort of . . . illuminated. You look . . . very symmetrical.

SIGMA: What—you wanna draw my picture?

[*They look at each other for a long moment.*]

JARED: Yes.

The Visit

Steven Schutzman

Dramatic

PHILIP: 8
JOSH: 10, PHILIP and CARL's brother
CARL: 14, PHILIP and JOSH's brother

PHILIP, JOSH, and CARL are sitting on the stoop of their grandparents' house, on a visit with their parents. Grandma's mind is going.

PHILIP: That's weird, making us sit out here like this.

JOSH: Big powwow.

PHILIP: I hope Grandma doesn't mix our names up again. That was so weird.

CARL: More sad, I'd say.

PHILIP: Yeah.

JOSH: So what were you laughing for?

PHILIP: Shut up.

JOSH: Well, don't laugh at Grandma.

PHILIP: I wasn't. [*To* CARL.] Is she ever going to be the same as she was again?

CARL: No.

PHILIP: Oh.

CARL: I've been reading up on it, online.

PHILIP: Oh.

CARL: It doesn't get better. It just gets worse.

PHILIP: Oh.

CARL: But if she does mix up our names again, Josh— don't correct her like you did.

PHILIP: Yeah.

JOSH: Don't worry. I won't. I don't want to be him again.

PHILIP: I don't want to be you either, numb nut.

CARL: Just ignore him, Philip.

JOSH: What's a "numb nut," Philip?

PHILIP: Who cares?

JOSH: See what I mean? He just says things.

CARL: And Philip, don't ask her for another soda like she didn't just give you one.

PHILIP: I just wanted to see what would happen.

JOSH: Right.

PHILIP: I did.

JOSH: Wittle baby of da family never do anything wrong.

CARL: Stop it, the two of you. This is not a good time.

PHILIP: Wait. I do too know. "Numb" is like all tingly, like when your foot goes to sleep, and "nut" is a crazy person. "Numb nut"—a tingly crazy person, like you.

JOSH: See, he's absurd.

PHILIP: What's absurd, Josh?

JOSH: Get away from me.

CARL: Just don't correct Grandma, okay?

JOSH: Grandpa's always correcting her.

CARL: He can't help it. It embarrasses him. And does it do any good? No. It just makes her feel bad and everyone else feel bad because she feels bad.

JOSH: So what am I supposed to do, just be called wrong?

CARL: Do what Dad does: "Go with the flow," like he says. If she says the plants are singing to her, ask her what the song is.

PHILIP: That is so weird.

CARL: Just don't correct her anymore. You saw how she got.

JOSH: Okay.

CARL: Music is important to her now, like to her mind. Why do you think Dad brings his guitar when we come over?

JOSH: Boring. [*Singing.*] "How many roads must a man walk down . . ."

CARL: That was a song from her childhood . . . a memory . . .

JOSH: Boring.

CARL: It's good and . . .

JOSH: Boring.

CARL: He's trying. At least, he's trying.

PHILIP: Yeah, Josh.

JOSH: What's a "numb nut," Philip?

PHILIP: What's absurd, Josh?

CARL: [*Loud and startling.*] SHE'S DAD'S MOM LIKE OUR MOM IS OUR MOM. [*Beat. Beat. Quietly:*] She's Dad's mom like our mom is our mom.

[*The three sit in silence on the stoop.*]

You Have to Wear Green on Tuesdays

Deanna Alisa Ableser

Dramatic

GIRL: 11 to 13; average looking, dressed in a trendy fashion.
BOY: 11 to 13; average looking, dressed in sporty clothes.

The BOY *and* GIRL *come out and stand center stage and address the audience.*

GIRL: It's not the divorce itself that really bugged me . . .

BOY: I mean, they were fighting all the time anyway . . .

GIRL: So it's really much better off that they're apart . . .

BOY: And I do get to enjoy the time I spend with each of them . . .

GIRL: But this commuting is really getting to me . . .

BOY: I spend more hours in the car going from Mom to Dad's place and back. Really doesn't put me in the best mood.

GIRL: Yeah. My mom lives in San Diego and my dad lives in Santa Barbara. I spend every other weekend at my dad's house. Let's see . . . four hours each way . . . back and forth . . . it's a big waste of everyone's time and it really is starting to get on my nerves.

BOY: [*Very irritated.*] And they just expect me to sit quietly and deal with it. I mean, it's not so bad when you're a little kid . . . you can sit and watch your little baby videos. But, I've got friends to hang out with, go skateboarding with, catch a movie with . . . I've got a life and I'm not really enjoying this getting shuffled back and forth.

GIRL: [*Very irritated.*] And let's not even get into the fighting over who knows what's best for "the kid." Mom always thinks she knows what's best for me and Dad always has to get the last word. They can't agree on anything and I'm ending up getting messed over.

[BOY *and* GIRL *turn toward each other. They mimic their parents.*]

BOY: I think he'd be better off in boarding school. He just can't seem to behave himself. Every day I get another phone call from the school about his behavior. I'm tired of it! He just needs to be shipped off to boarding school to get his act together.

GIRL: He's fine! What are you talking about? Don't you see . . . it's all your fault anyway! He behaves fine when he is with me. You're just a lousy dad. Hanging out in bars all the time!

BOY: Hanging out in bars! You're such a lousy liar! I spend hours at two jobs just trying to raise enough money for child support and you . . .

GIRL: Child support?! How ridiculous can you get! I can't even tell you how many times you've been late for child support . . .

BOY: Would you just be quiet already?! I'm so tired of your constant yelling and bickering! Why don't you just get a real job and stop "exploring your options"?

[GIRL *and* BOY *face audience again.*]

GIRL: And that's just one type of fight. Then there's the holiday deal.

BOY: Mom wants me for Christmas.

GIRL: Dad wants me for Christmas.

BOY: Is it an even- or odd-numbered year? Do I go with Dad? Is it Mom's year?

GIRL: I think it's getting to be a bit ridiculous. I mean, I'm not a master scheduler. Don't use me to figure out where I should or should not be at whatever time you're thinking about.

BOY: For goodness sakes, *you're* the adults. Figure it out. It's bad enough I don't get to spend the holidays with all of my family and in one place, but at least figure out where I'm supposed to be . . .

GIRL: But please . . . through it all . . . remember . . .

BOY: I'm not a toy . . .

GIRL: Or a plaything to be tossed around . . .

BOY: I'm a kid . . .

GIRL: With feelings . . .

BOY: And lots of friends . . .

GIRL: So, when you're making your schedules . . .

BOY: And figuring out child support . . .

GIRL: And trying to decide what's best for me . . .

BOY: Just take a second and try to remember that.

[GIRL *and* BOY *high-five each other.*]

Play Sources and Acknowledgments

FRANKENFISH © 2014 by Steven Schutzman. Reprinted by permission of Steven Schutzman. For performance rights, contact Steven Schutzman

(sschutzman@gmail.com).

GATHERING BLUE © 2013 by Eric Coble. Reprinted by permission of Kate Navin, The Gersh Agency. For performance rights, contact Dramatic Publishing Co.

(www.dramaticpublishing.com).

GET TO THE POINT © 2014 by Fran Handman. Reprinted by permission of Fran Handman. For performance rights, contact Fran Handman

(franhand4@aol.com).

THE GREAT KITTEN CAPER © 2015 by Mark Lambeck. Reprinted by permission of Mark Lambeck. For performance rights, contact Mark Lambeck

(markray516@gmail.com).

GREEN CRAYON © 2013 by Rebecca Gorman O'Neill. Reprinted by permission of Rebecca Gorman O'Neill. For performance rights, contact Rebecca Gorman O'Neill

(gormanreb@aol.com).

HAPPY WORST DAY EVER © 2015 by Arlene Hutton. Reprinted by permission of Arlene Hutton, c/o Beth Lincks. For performance rights, contact Dramatic Publishing Co.

(www.dramaticpublishing.com).

HAVE A HOPPY HOLIDAY © 2015 by Scot Walker. Reprinted by permission of Scot Walker. For performance rights, contact Scot Walker

(scotwalker2004@yahoo.com).

THE HOUSE OF BROKEN DREAMS © 2015 by Carol Costa. Reprinted by permission of Carol Costa. For performance rights, contact Carol Costa

(carolcosta62003@yahoo.com).

Other Monologue and Scene Books

Best Contemporary Monologues for Kids Ages 7-15
edited by Lawrence Harbison
9781495011771 .... $16.99

Best Contemporary Monologues for Men 18-35
edited by Lawrence Harbison
9781480369610 .... $16.99

Best Contemporary Monologues for Women 18-35
edited by Lawrence Harbison
9781480369627 .... $16.99

Best Monologues from The Best American Short Plays, Volume Three
edited by William W. Demastes
9781480397408 .... $19.99

Best Monologues from The Best American Short Plays, Volume Two
edited by William W. Demastes
9781480385481 .... $19.99

Best Monologues from The Best American Short Plays, Volume One
edited by William W. Demastes
9781480331556 .... $19.99

Childsplay
A Collection of Scenes and Monologues for Children
edited by Kerry Muir
9780879101886 .... $16.99

Duo!: The Best Scenes for Mature Actors
edited by Stephen Fife
9781480360204 .... $19.99

Duo!: The Best Scenes for Two for the 21st Century
edited by Joyce E. Henry, Rebecca Dunn Jaroff, and Bob Shuman
9781557837028 .... $19.99

Duo!: Best Scenes for the 90's
edited by John Horvath, Lavonne Mueller, and Jack Temchin
9781557830302 .... $18.99

In Performance: Contemporary Monologues for Teens
by JV Mercanti
9781480396616 .... $16.99

In Performance: Contemporary Monologues for Men and Women Late Teens to Twenties
by JV Mercanti
9781480331570 .... $18.99

In Performance: Contemporary Monologues for Men and Women Late Twenties to Thirties
by JV Mercanti
9781480367470 .... $16.99

Men's Comedic Monologues That Are Actually Funny
edited by Alisha Gaddis
9781480396814 .... $14.99

The Monologue Audition
A Practical Guide for Actors
by Karen Kohlhaas
9780879102913 .... $22.99

One on One: The Best Men's Monologues for the 21st Century
edited by Joyce E. Henry, Rebecca Dunn Jaroff, and Bob Shuman
9781557837011 .... $18.99

One on One: The Best Women's Monologues for the 21st Century
edited by Joyce E. Henry, Rebecca Dunn Jaroff, and Bob Shuman
9781557837004 .... $18.99

One on One: Playing with a Purpose
Monologues for Kids Ages 7-15
edited by Stephen Fife and Bob Shuman with contributing editors Eloise Rollins-Fife and Marit Shuman
9781557838414 .... $16.99

One on One: The Best Monologues for Mature Actors
edited by Stephen Fife
9781480360198 .... $19.99

Scenes and Monologues of Spiritual Experience from the Best Contemporary Plays
edited by Roger Ellis
9731480331563 .... $19.99

Scenes and Monologues from Steinberg/ATCA New Play Award Finalists, 2008-2012
edited by Bruce Burgun
9781476868783 .... $19.99

Soliloquy!
The Shakespeare Monologues
edited by Michael Earley and Philippa Keil
9780936839783 Men's
Edition $12.99
9780936839790 Women's
Edition $14.95

Teen Boys' Comedic Monologues That Are Actually Funny
edited by Alisha Gaddis
9781480396791 .... $14.99

Teens Girls' Comedic Monologues That Are Actually Funny
edited by Alisha Gaddis
9781480396807 .... $14.99

Women's Comedic Monologues That Are Actually Funny
edited by Alisha Gaddis
9781480360426 .... $14.99

Prices, contents, and availability subject to change without notice.